Primary English Curriculum Guide

CHRISTINE MOORCROFT
and RAY BARKER

David Fulton Publishers
London

David Fulton Publishers Ltd
Ormond House, 26–27 Boswell Street, London WC1N 3JZ.

www.fultonpublishers.co.uk

First published in Great Britain by David Fulton Publishers 2000

British Library Cataloguing in Publication Data
A catalogue record for this book is available from the British Library

ISBN 1-85346-723-5

Typeset by Elite Typesetting Techniques, Eastleigh, Hampshire
Printed in Great Britain by Bell and Bain Ltd, Glasgow

Contents

Introduction

Teaching English

The purpose of this curriculum guide is to help student teachers and newly qualified teachers to make a start on learning how to become competent teachers of English. Despite the emphasis given in training courses to the teaching of English, newly qualified teachers often feel under-prepared for it and frequently mention their concerns about this. These concerns can be partly explained by a general lack of confidence in this key area and partly by widespread media and political criticism of the teaching of literacy. It is also because it is often difficult for a student to make the connection between observation of key teaching strategies and his or her own personal practice.

Prior to the introduction of the Literacy Hour, class teachers with a student have often recognised that it is difficult to manage reading in addition to classroom organisation and curriculum planning. Welcoming the presence of students, they themselves have concentrated on reading and numeracy for small groups of pupils. Student teachers, however, have thus been deprived of valuable practical experience in the teaching of reading.

More than the National Literacy Strategy

Learning how to teach English is more than simply becoming familiar with central government publications. Although this is important, it is neither the starting nor finishing point of acquiring the necessary skills to manage, stimulate and teach pupils to become literate members of our society. In *The Implementation of the National Literacy Strategy* (DfEE, 1997) the Literacy Task Force identified the role of the key agents involved in raising standards of literacy. The National Literacy Strategy resource materials provide exemplars of how reading and writing can be taught.

The *Framework for Teaching* was based on the National Literacy Project (NLP). This was a central government initiative, initially directed at 10 local education authorities, where literacy standards were considered to be poor in some schools. The authorities had to bid for funding and the successful ones received additional resources for a limited number of schools. The majority chose schools where literacy levels fell well below national averages. The teaching and learning programme devised by the NLP and disseminated by specially trained project workers started from the perceived need for these schools to have a systematic approach to the teaching of reading across the school, and a belief that certain teaching strategies were more effective than others.

It is perhaps worth remembering, at this point, that many primary schools already had successful, detailed and practical schemes of work for literacy in line with the National Curriculum requirements. Initial documentation from the NLS indicated that, provided they could produce a school literacy plan to show how externally-set literacy targets could be met, they could continue with these programmes. Later documentation made this less concessionary and the implication of the *Framework for Teaching* was that most, if not all, schools would adopt the same framework. This presented many challenges for schools:

- Many of the ideas for the National Literacy Strategy were drawn from the teaching of literacy in Australia, New Zealand and the USA where the whole morning might be spent on teaching literacy.

- The *Framework* and the accompanying INSET were introduced at breakneck speed involving limited opportunity for wider discussion of teaching strategies.

- Early Learning Goals do not fit neatly into the NLS proposals for reception children.

Central government's response to help schools included:

- a huge injection of funding to support professional development for teachers and governors, including funding for the appointment of literacy consultants in LEAs;

- additional funding for resources;

- lifting of the statutory requirements for all the foundation subjects apart from ICT (Information and Communication Technology);

- an optimistic educational ethos that schools *could* make a significant difference to children's learning.

Initial Teacher Training and Continued Professional Development

The National Literacy Strategy required initial teacher training institutions to ensure that student teachers were confident about their knowledge and skills in the teaching of literacy. Linked to this was a requirement that all primary teachers should take part in a programme of planned professional development in the teaching of literacy. The designation of 1998/9 as the National Year of Reading and its contribution as the National Reading Campaign highlighted the importance of examining the ways in which schools organised the teaching of reading, in particular those which had already organised their teaching round the Literacy Hour.

Definitions of literacy

The National Literacy Project defined the literate primary child as one who should:

- read and write with confidence, fluency and understanding;

- be interested in books, read with enjoyment and evaluate and justify preferences;

- know and understand a range of genres in fiction and poetry, and understand and be familiar with some of the ways in which narratives are structured through basic literary ideas of setting, character and plot;

- understand and be able to use a range of non-fiction texts;

- be able to orchestrate a full range of reading cues (phonic, graphic, syntactic, contextual) to monitor and self-correct his or her own reading;

- plan, draft, revise and edit his or her own writing;

- have an interest in words and word meanings, and a growing vocabulary;

- understand the sound and spelling system and use this to read and spell accurately;

- have fluent and legible handwriting.

The *Framework for Teaching* laid these out in a slightly different order and added that the literate pupil should also:

- have a suitable technical vocabulary through which to understand and discuss his or her reading and writing;

- through reading and writing, develop his or her powers of imagination, inventiveness and critical awareness.

The 2000 National Curriculum document breaks reading and writing down into Knowledge, Skills and Understanding. It is recommended that you keep a reading journal in which you make systematic notes about the children's books you read:
author, date, publisher, genre, any special theme or message, potential for developing children's learning in specific areas of English.

How best to use this book

To obtain the maximum benefit from this book you need to spend time in a school, preferably on an organised attachment. You will also need access to the *Literacy Training Pack*, which was supplied to all schools.

The materials provided for all schools in the *Literacy Training Pack* are used as the basic framework for this English course. The DfEE no longer produces the pack but all schools have it and will be willing to lend different sections of it to trainee teachers.

In this guide, a limited number of texts are 'recommended readers' and should be purchased in order to provide background reading. A more comprehensive reading list is set out in pp 76 and 77, divided into 'General background reading', 'Teaching resources for the classroom' and 'Poetry Anthologies'. More detailed guidance about the objectives and support materials (books, resources and audio–visual aids) for each chapter is set out in pp 78–95.

In all these lists, 'recommended readers' are identified by bold type and often specific chapter or page references are given to locate information about the individual chapter topics and tasks. These are the books which you should consider purchasing or borrowing from a library.

Chapter 1

English in the primary school and its place in the curriculum

THEMES

The development of the teaching of English in primary schools; the effects of research and of pressures from Government.

Task 1: The influences of research

New research leads to new approaches in the teaching of English (and other subjects). Some of these approaches seem to be completely at odds with one another but, as Wray and Medwell (1998) point out, a great deal of knowledge has been amassed about the ways in which children learn.

Graham and Kelly's (2000) description of the changes in one teacher's methods during the course of her career illustrates the influences on, and changes in, academic thought from the 1930s to the 1980s. Many teachers, however, do not undertake courses leading to higher degrees, and so their views about children's learning are largely influenced by their own school experiences and by their initial training.

Can you remember how you yourself were taught to read and write? It would be helpful to jot down your memories. For example, were you taught to read mainly through the use of phonics – or through the 'look and say' method? Did you work your way through a reading scheme – or did your school favour the use of 'real books'? When you were required to write an account of, say, your work in science, were you given a structure around which to write it – or did the class copy the teacher's account? Did you, for example, learn lists of spellings and have regular tests on them?

Your written memories will help you to place your own education into the context of the educational views and theories which were prevalent, or fashionable, at the time.

 What assumptions about the learning process and which research findings influenced the ways in which you were taught English?

Consider your notes about your own schooldays in relation to the theories of learning about which you have read.

 What assumptions about the learning process and which research findings have influenced the ways in which English is now being taught in primary schools?

Consider some of the methods of teaching English about which you have read and which you have observed in schools and relate each of them to a particular school of thought propounded by researchers.

Task 2: The influences of government pressure

Before the Education Reform Act 1988 the only compulsory subject which had to be taught in every school was religious education (Education Act 1944); it was also the only subject from which parents could withdraw their children and which individual teachers could decline to teach.

When the government proposed a National Curriculum to coincide with the Education Reform Act 1988, the three 'core subjects' it included were English, mathematics and science. These were to be given substantially more time than the seven 'foundation subjects' of design technology, information technology, history, geography, art, music and physical education, with religious education based on locally-agreed syllabuses. The order in which the ten subjects are listed gives an indication of their perceived importance. In the early 1980s British industry and British children's attainment in science had compared unfavourably with those of other developed countries, and the first major initiative in testing children's attainment in science was undertaken; for the first time, science was given the same status as English.

 The contents of the primary school curriculum and the priority given to each subject have undergone changes. How have the views of employers, the media and the government influenced these changes?

Task 3: The National Curriculum

Subject working parties for the National Curriculum were set up in the mid-1980s to advise the government about what should be taught within each area of the curriculum for children aged 5–16. In 1991 the first statutory orders of the National Curriculum set out what schools were required to teach children at each Key Stage, and how much time should be spent on each subject. Their purpose was to standardise what children all over England and Wales were taught. The Secretary of State for Education at the time, Kenneth Baker, claimed that it would enable children who moved from one school to another, or even from one part of the country to another, to continue with the same curriculum. In 1995 the National Curriculum was revised, with the intention of retaining it without change until 2000, and that is what has happened.

 What conflicts might there be between the views of teachers about the ways in which children learn to read and write and the requirements of the National Curriculum?

Look in 'The National Curriculum for Primary Teachers in England' www.nc.uk.net.
What are the three attainment targets for English?
Make notes on each one for your chosen Key Stage.
Also view Sequence 1, Video 1 of 'The Literacy Training Pack' (DfEE 1998).

● You should now have an insight into the background of the diverse approaches to the teaching of English and the events leading to the introduction of the National Curriculum.

Chapter 2

Story

THEME
The importance of stories to children's language development.

Task 1: How to choose a good story

Many students and newly-qualified teachers find choosing stories to read to and with children, or for children to read independently, a daunting task. It is natural to begin with stories which you have heard read in schools or have had recommended to you, but this can be very limiting. You can develop your story-choosing skills and thereby learn to trust your own judgement. It will help if you examine two well-known children's stories which have been given the seal of approval by experts.

What makes a children's fiction book good?

Read each of the two award-winning fiction books (see p79) and then make brief notes about how you felt while you were reading it and how you reacted: for example, did it bring a smile to your face or even make you laugh aloud, did it bring tears to your eyes or even make you cry, did it make you feel uneasy, did it create any feelings of revulsion, fear or excitement?

After you have made a note of your overriding reactions and feelings re-read the book, or the parts of it which affected you the most, and make more systematic notes about the pages, paragraphs or even words which caused any of the feelings. You might find that there are other feelings to add to your original list.

Make a note of your level of motivation to finish the books, perhaps on a scale from finishing it only in order to complete this task, to being unable to put it down. Make notes of anything about the books which you think would appeal to children.

Task 2: Encouraging children to read for enjoyment

Teachers need to take care that the books they read with children do not become mere vehicles for teaching reading and writing skills. Many of the lessons shown on the Literacy Training Pack videos and the Activity Resource Sheets, and in the lesson plans suggested by Wray & Medwell (1998), with their emphasis on the teaching of text-, sentence- and word-level skills, might lose sight of the enjoyment of a good story. Many of us have heard children say to their teacher who was diligently pointing out the title page, the name of the author and illustrator, the inside cover, and so on, "Miss/Sir, can we have the story now?" We need to teach children these things, but be careful not to spoil a story with the teaching of skills.

How can you arouse the children's interest in a story?

Describe what you would do to arouse children's interest in one of the two books you read for Task 1. Graham & Kelly (2000) give some suggestions, and you could also consider the following:
- *re-writing the blurb for the children to read;*
- *displaying a poster about the book (ask the publisher for one), a copy of the opening sentence or another sentence or paragraph; questions related to the story: for example, "What makes you feel better if you are afraid of the dark?" or "What do you see in your dreams?"*

Task 3: Children's learning at text level

Each of the two stories you read for Task 2 lends itself to particular aspects of text-level work. These help children to identify the features which made it a good story, while at the same time they learn about the features of stories which help them, in turn, to write good stories of their own.

Describe the whole-class and group text-level activities (for reading and writing) which could be planned in relation to one of the two books above. These would not necessarily all take place in one lesson or even a series of lessons

Refer to the Activity Resource Sheets from the Literacy Training Pack (either Module 4 [Key Stage 1] or Module 5 [Key Stage 2]). Identify the National Literacy Strategy text-level reference for each activity and describe what you would do and the types of responses you would expect from children.

As a starting point you might find it helpful to complete Figure 2.1 or 2.2, which are not intended for children's use. Ideas from them can then be selected to form the basis of text-level work with children, but not all in one lesson or series of lessons.

● You should now have an explicit understanding of what characterises a good story for children and an awareness of the ways in which you can encourage children to enjoy reading.
● You should also be able to plan specific text-level learning activities which can be developed from stories.

Figure 2.1 *Can't You Sleep, Little Bear?*

Repeated elements of the story:
Repeated words in the story:
Questions which invite the children to tell or write additional episodes for the story:
What is your favourite moment from the story, and what do you like about it?
Describe the character of Big Bear:
Describe the character of Little Bear:

Figure 2.2 *Skellig*

Describe the setting of the story and identify what it makes the reader think might happen:
Which details in the description of the setting are the most important, and why?
What might Mina say to "Rasputin", Michael's science teacher, and what might he say to her?
What might "Doctor Death" say to Skellig and what might Skellig do or say in return?
What facts do you know about Skellig, and what ideas do you have about him?
What would you like to ask Skellig?
What answer do you think he would give?

Chapter 3

The National Literacy Strategy

THEME
An overview of the National Literacy Strategy.

Task 1: The introduction of the National Literacy Strategy

Governments, local education authorities, schools and teachers have always wanted the children for whose education they are responsible to become literate and have worked towards this aim but, even after the National Curriculum was introduced, it was found that children's attainment in all subjects varied from school to school. The OFSTED (Office for Standards in Education) inspections of schools, introduced in 1994, provided an enormous increase in the amount of information available about children's attainment at different ages.

Most attention was paid to this variation in attainment in literacy and numeracy. However, as well as the variation itself, the government was concerned about the low levels of attainment in literacy and numeracy in many schools.

How is the National Literacy Strategy different from previous Government advice issued about the teaching of English?

Consider the nature of the advice given to schools (its tone and how specific it is in terms of content, teaching methods and timing).

Task 2: The Literacy Hour

In September 1998 all but a handful of schools in England incorporated the daily Literacy Hour into their timetables. This was not intended to increase the time spent teaching English but, for many teachers, it did change the organisation and content of their lessons. A greater emphasis was placed on direct teaching and on high-quality teacher interaction with a greater number of children during the time allocated to English. In order to achieve this high-quality interaction, teachers had to help their pupils to develop self-help strategies so that they would not need to interrupt the teacher's guided reading and writing activities with other groups. This, however, is not the main *purpose* of independent work, which has intrinsic benefits in developing children's ability to work independently at a high level.

For the Literacy Hour to function properly, teachers need to organise their classes carefully. Figure 3.1 lists some methods of organisation and leaves space for you to add others as you come across them.

Figure 3.1 Managing the Literacy Hour

Organisation	Strategies	Equipment
Task management boards. Task cards. Using a timer. Storage of books to enable easy retrieval for both teacher and children.	Setting acceptable levels of noise. Using methods of reducing noise which have an immediate effect. Rewarding performance in the Literacy Hour. Behaviour contracts. Routines which enable the children to locate and use information without asking the teacher.	Carefully prepared and labelled resource boxes for the class and for groups. 'Finished work' trays. Signs to show which groups of children are working alone and which are working with the teacher.

In what ways have the methods of many teachers remained unchanged and what changes have teachers had to make in order to teach the Literacy Hour?

Consider classroom organisation:
- *whole-class, group and individual teaching;*
- *mixed-ability teaching and differentiation;*
- *strategies for encouraging independent work and avoiding interruptions while teaching another group;*
- *materials and other resources, including the range and type of texts and the ways in which they are presented and used;*
- *the links between English and other subjects.*

Task 3: The structure of the Literacy Hour

The Literacy Hour has a definite structure which requires careful planning by the teacher. This structure ensures a balance of whole-class teaching, differentiated group teaching and individual work by children, the timing of all of which is prescribed. During the hour, work covers whole-class shared reading and writing; whole-class focused teaching (phonics, vocabulary, spelling, grammar, punctuation and handwriting); group teaching (guided reading or guided writing, independent reading or independent writing tasks) and a whole-class plenary session (for reviewing, reflecting and consolidating teaching points and for sharing work covered during the lesson).

Throughout the Literacy Hour *all* of the teacher's time must be spent in direct teaching.

 Complete Figure 3.2 (taken from Literacy Training Pack Module 1, Teacher's Notes, page 5) to show what one teacher (and class) which you have observed did during the Literacy Hour.

Include
- *the name and genre of the shared text and the context or topic of shared writing, focused word work or sentence work and independent work;*
- *the teaching points of the introductory session, focused word or sentence work and independent work;*
- *the strategies used by the children if they needed help during their independent work;*
- *what the teacher did during the plenary session to review and consolidate the teaching points.*

● You should now understand the way in which the Literacy Hour has been incorporated into the primary school curriculum and be aware of its impact on the teaching and learning of English.
● You should also be familiar with the structure and content of the Literacy Hour and the purpose of each part of it.

Figure 3.2 (from *Literacy Training Pack, Module 1, Teacher's Notes*, p5)

Class organisation for the Literacy Hour		
15 mins	Shared reading or writing (Whole class)	
15 mins	Word or sentence work (Whole class)	
20 mins	Guided reading or writing (Ability grouping: the teacher works with at least two groups)	
20 mins	Independent work (Group work) (Simultaneous with guided reading or writing)	
10 mins	Plenary (Whole class)	

Chapter 4

Development in reading

THEMES
An overview of the theories of learning and approaches to the teaching of reading in primary schools, including the methods of the Literacy Hour.

Task 1: Theories of learning

How do children learn? Wray & Medwell (1998) give a succinct overview of the key ideas which have emerged from theories of learning: it is an interaction between what the learner knows and what is to be learned; a social process; and a metacognitive process. They describe principles for teaching derived from these ideas, and translate these principles into action in a 'Model for teaching'. This describes two approaches to reading where the procedures involved at first look similar, but which take place in a different order: reciprocal reading (summarising, questioning, clarifying and predicting) and meta-reading (predicting, clarifying, questioning and summarising). The main difference between the approaches is that, in the second, the reader makes explicit what he or she is trying to do.

You should be able to find some links between this model of teaching and the approaches suggested in the *National Literacy Strategy Framework for Teaching*.

Which parts of Wray & Medwell's 'Model for teaching' have you observed in the Literacy Hour?

In the lessons shown on the video (Literacy Training Pack Video 1, Module 1, Sequences 2-5) find two examples each of reciprocal teaching (the procedure of summarising, questioning, clarifying and predicting in order to understand the text) and of meta-reading (the process whereby the reader is aware of, and can describe, the procedures of predicting, clarifying, questioning and summarising, and can say what he or she is trying to do and why).

Having found the examples, describe what the teacher and children were doing.

Task 2: Learning to read

How do children learn to read? It would be ideal to have a definitive answer – an answer which would produce a single infallible method of teaching children to read. Many methods have been used, some of them based on conflicting views, but all based on research into, and observation of, children learning to read.

You may be asking yourself how a knowledge of methods which were popular in the past could help you to teach children to read now, and in the future. Bear in mind that most theories and methods are not completely rejected and that new research simply adds to the accumulating body of knowledge. Look for the ways in which past methods have become incorporated into more recent ones.

Figure 4.1 Using the 'searchlight' model

Text (details of the book, and the page reference.)
Phonic knowledge
Knowledge of the context
Grammatical knowledge
Word recognition and graphic knowledge

Five significant methods of teaching reading which have influenced the ways in which reading is now taught are the 'phonic', 'look and say', 'language experience', 'miscue analysis' and 'real books' approaches.

What advantages and disadvantages are there in each method of teaching children to read?

Consider the ways in which the 'phonic', 'look and say', 'language experience', 'miscue analysis' and 'real books' approaches can help children to learn to read, and the problems they might face if only one approach were used.

Task 3: The 'searchlight model'

The *National Literacy Strategy Framework for Teaching* provides a model (the 'searchlight model') which describes four strategies for making sense of text ('searchlights'): phonic (sounds and spelling); grammatical knowledge; word-recognition and graphic knowledge; and knowledge of context.

How can the searchlight model be translated into action?

Choose a passage from a children's book (perhaps one of those you have described in your Reading Journal) and give examples of the ways in which a child might use each 'searchlight' to read and understand it. Use Figure 4.1 to structure your examples.

● You should now have insights into the background of the diverse approaches to the teaching of reading, the research upon which they were founded and their influence on the methods advocated in the *National Literacy Strategy Framework for Teaching*.

Chapter 5

Shared reading

THEME
Shared reading and its place in the Literacy Hour. This chapter deals mainly with fiction, since poetry, drama and non-fiction texts are addressed later in the course.

Task 1: The purpose of a shared text

'Big Books' are well-established resources in Key Stage 1 classrooms, but were not common in Key Stage 2, particularly for the older children, before the 1990s. They enable a group of children, or even a whole class, to read the same text simultaneously. But 'Big Books' are not the only resources which do this – equally useful are multiple copies of texts, and extracts copied on to paper or overhead transparencies. Many Key Stage 2 teachers have grave reservations about sitting children on the floor to read a 'Big Book' together.

At Key Stage 1 teachers should model reading strategies and draw attention to features of the text. They should also use shared reading sessions to teach children about the conventions used in books, such as 'title page' and 'cover'.

At Key Stage 2 teachers should develop the children's reading strategies and analyse elements of the text in terms of narrative structure: for example, plot and character.

A shared text can be used to teach text-, sentence- and word-level skills, but the teacher needs to ensure that this teaching does not spoil the children's enjoyment of the text.

 What do the teachers of Key Stage 1 children do during shared reading and how is the shared text used ?

Consider what the teachers do during the video sequences (Literacy Training Pack Video 2, Modules 4, Sequences 1–2 and 5, Sequences 1 and 4). *Use Figure 5.1 to structure your responses.*

 What do the teachers of Key Stage 2 children do during shared reading and how is the shared text used ?

Consider how the Year 3 teacher uses the 'Big Book', Rumpelstiltskin, *to investigate traditional story language and to discuss main and recurring characters. Also look at how the Year 6 teacher uses the story of Theseus to encourage the children to articulate personal responses to literature and to identify key features of plot structure.*

Figure 5.1 Shared reading observation (from DfEE (1998) *Literacy Training Pack, Module 4: Shared and Guided Reading at Pre-Key Stage 1 and Key Stage 1, Teacher's Notes*, p 11)

Teacher's role	Video Sequence 2 Extract 1	Video Sequence 2 Extract 2
To read the text *with* (not merely *to*) the class.		
To demonstrate how to read, including the use of correspondence between sounds and words and directionality of text, and to teach basic concepts, eg, book, page, line, word, letter.		
To teach and practise phonic and word recognition skills in context.		
To identify sentence structure and punctuation.		
To teach reading strategies: monitoring and checking reading for sense; identifying and correcting errors; inferring unknown words from surrounding text and confirming them by reference to their spelling patterns.		
To accommodate a range of reading ability in the class by differentiating questions which enable children of different abilities to participate at an appropriate level.		
Other teaching points:		

Task 2: Planning for shared reading

Long-term planning should ensure that the children will experience the *range* of texts recommended in the *Framework for Teaching*. Within that range the teacher needs to identify the most useful texts for shared reading. The texts chosen should hold the children's interest, and the language should be well within their comprehension level, but above the level at which most of them can read independently.

Your Reading Journal will provide a valuable and time-saving source of reference throughout your teaching career, especially if the texts you include are accompanied by accurate notes about their level of difficulty, children's responses to them (if you have used them or seen them in use) and, of course, the opportunities which they present for teaching text-, sentence- and word-level skills.

 For either Key Stage 1 or Key Stage 2, choose a fiction text and identify the aspects of text-, sentence- and word-level work in the *Framework for Teaching* for which it could be used.

Consider the age-group for which the text is suitable and the term in which it would be most useful. Make a note of the high-frequency words in the text.

● You should now understand the essential characteristics of shared reading, be able to make informed choices about the texts and recognise the reading skills which can be taught from them.

Chapter 6

Guided reading

THEME
Guided reading and its place in the Literacy Hour.

Task 1: The purpose of guided reading

Some of the research which you considered in Chapter 3 (Wray & Medwell, 1998) showed the importance of supported activity during the learning process and noted that this stage of supported learning is often neglected. Teachers tend to move too quickly from giving children a great deal of help to asking them to work unaided. Guided reading can provide the bridge between the two.

During a guided reading session children should achieve some of the text-, sentence- and word-level skills described in the *Framework for Teaching*.

Which of the objectives of the *Framework for Teaching* do the children meet during the lessons shown in the video sequences?

Look for evidence of the skills described for the autumn term's work for each of the year groups shown. You should combine the recording of this with that of Task 2. Write on Figure 6.1.

Task 2: The guided reading session

The main difference between shared reading and guided reading is that, in the former, the teacher models reading strategies for the children, whereas, in the latter, he or she helps the children to use these strategies themselves. Different texts should be used for shared and guided reading. A text chosen for guided reading should be at a level where children (grouped by ability) are able to read 95% of it independently. As in shared reading, consideration should be given to providing a range of genres.

During the 20 minutes group work/independent work session the teacher works intensively with one or two small groups of children for 20 minutes. One of its advantages over individual reading is the increased teaching time which each child can receive: in *Video 2 (Literacy Training Pack)*, John Stannard, the Director of the National Literacy Strategy, pointed out that the Literacy Hour enabled this time to be increased fourfold.

What do the teachers of Key Stage 1 children do during guided reading and what is the main focus of each session?

Consider the sequence of teaching: introducing the book, structuring independent reading, returning to the discussion of the text and following up the lesson.

Figure 6.1 Guided and independent reading: notes on the videos (from DfEE (1998) *Literacy Training Pack, Module 5: Shared and Guided Reading at Key Stage 2, Teacher's Notes*, pp 14-15)

Year 4 *The Frog who wanted to be a Horse*	**Year 6 Literature Circle:** *Meteorite Spoon*
Objectives	
Y4 T1: To identify the main characteristics of the key characters, drawing on the text to justify views.	Y6 T3: To use a reading journal effectively to raise and refine personal responses to a text.
Reading skills	
Match with objectives	
Teaching strategies	

What do the teachers of Key Stage 2 children do during guided reading and what is the main focus of each session?

Consider the reading skills which each teacher is aiming to develop, the teaching strategies used and the extent to which the lesson matches its objectives (see Figure 6.1, which you can use to structure your responses).

Task 3: Independent work

In Chapter 3 you came across some of the methods which teachers use for organising their classes for independent work, guided reading and guided writing and for helping the children to work within this system. Children who are working independently should not merely be 'occupied' while the teacher concentrates on one group; they should be engaged in meaningful reading or writing activities. There are many useful published materials to support independent activities (see **Further Reading** [Appendix 1]).

 Choose an activity from a published source and explain, briefly, how you would use it.

Consider the year group for which the material is suitable and which text-, word- or sentence-level work it supports. Include how you would introduce it and how you would review the children's work during the plenary session.

● You should now understand the essential characteristics of guided reading and how a class should be organised for guided reading and independent work.
● You should also be able to select activities to support independent word-, sentence- or text-level work on given topics.

Chapter 7
Development in writing

Task 1: Genres of text

Children need to *read* texts from different genres in order to learn how to *write* them. Not every text will be prescribed in the school's curriculum statement – there is scope for teachers to develop and use their own subject knowledge.

For a school year of your choice, consider the range of texts to be read during each term. Collect as many non-book texts as possible which could be used as a basis for developing text-level work.

Your Reading Journal should help you to select examples of texts of each genre across the prescribed range. You can augment it with timetables, leaflets, advertisements, comics and photographs of texts like notices and signs.
Important features to note include:
- *the person in which the text is written;*
- *the tense in which it is written;*
- *its audience, its purpose and where it is intended to be read;*
- *whether or not it contains dialogue;*
- *the organisation of the text: paragraphs, bullets, headings, captions, alphabetical order, boxes, lines, keys, arrows, flow charts, diagrams, parentheses, footnotes, asterisks, appendices, glossary, index;*
- *whether the language is personal or impersonal, formal or informal;*
- *the length and complexity of the sentences;*
- *any use of poetic devices such as rhythm, rhyme, word-play;*
- *humour;*
- *the use of persuasion and argument.*

Task 2: The characteristic features of a genre

Children can learn to write in the styles of different genres by reading them and investigating the ways in which experts write. For example, to write a play-script, the children need not only to have read play-scripts but also to have investigated and, better still, discussed their text- and sentence-level features. They can identify the features of a script which make it different from other kinds of text. By going through the process you expect children to undertake, you will be better able to teach them.

Figure 7.1 Audience, purpose and context

Year ___ Term ___	**Audience**	**Purpose**	**Context**
Strand		Fiction	
Strand		Non-fiction	

What are the specific features of a play-script which make it different from narrative text?

(You can also carry out this activity with Year 4 children. It covers Term 1, Strand T5 of the National Literacy Strategy.)
Make a note of the special features of a play-script and write a list of 'rules' for writing a play-script. Read a piece of fiction which contains dialogue and, on a copy of part of it, mark the action and the dialogue in different colours. Then, following your rules for writing a play-script, convert the dialogue into a script. Make a note of any other information which is needed in addition to dialogue, and how it should be presented in a play-script: for example, the setting, the actions of the speakers and, if necessary, the way in which they speak.

Task 3: Purpose, context and audience

Children need to have a purpose, a context and an audience for their writing and these will affect its tone, language and structure. The National Literacy Strategy is specific. Within the writing strand of text-level work, purposes and contexts are suggested (and sometimes audiences) but at other times the audience can be inferred from the purpose and context: for example (in Reception Year), 'Pupils should be taught... to understand that writing can be used for a range of purposes, e.g. to send messages, record, inform and tell stories...'.

The teacher can make the purpose, context and audience explicit, even for the youngest children, by discussing where their writing will be displayed, kept, read or sent, for what it will be used, how it will be useful and who will read it. Real contexts for children's writing can be linked with work in other subjects: for example, instructions for making something they have designed and made, a letter to someone who is ill or a report of a scientific investigation (to be published in a class 'Science Journal').

Sometimes it is not possible to have a real purpose, context or audience for children's writing, but meaningful ones can be invented: for example, a letter to a character in a story, an epitaph for someone from history or a guide-book for aliens visiting the Earth (perhaps based on the *Dr Xargle* series by Jeanne Willis and Tony Ross).

Identify a suitable purpose, context and audience for all the fiction and non-fiction writing composition objectives of the National Literacy Strategy for one term in a school year of your choice.

Figure 7.1 will help you to structure your responses.

● You should now be able to select texts from different genres of writing which are suitable for a particular age-group and be aware of the possible purposes, contexts and audiences for children writing in those genres.

Chapter 8
Shared writing

THEME
Shared writing and its place in the Literacy Hour. This chapter deals mainly with fiction, since poetry, drama and non-fiction texts are addressed later.

Task 1: The value of shared writing and how teachers use it

Shared writing enables children to take part in a writing activity at a higher level than that which they could undertake alone. Graham & Kelly (1998, 19) note that, in shared writing, the teacher can set high expectations by placing the children in 'the zone of proximal knowledge' (Vygotsky), leading them into new skills which they cannot yet undertake independently. Shared writing should produce a text of which the contributors can be proud.

The essential teaching components of shared writing are the compositional aspects (structure and content) and the transcriptional aspects (spelling, punctuation, spacing and handwriting).

In shared writing, the teacher has to use strategies which help the children to work at this high level. The teacher asks for suggestions from the class, takes notes, acts as scribe, models writing skills, makes suggestions for editing the text, discusses the effects of the children's suggestions and leads the children through the writing and publishing process.

What do the teachers of Key Stage 1 children do during shared writing?

Consider what the teachers do during the video sequences (Literacy Training Pack Video 2), and use Figure 8.1 to structure your responses.

What does the teacher of Key Stage 2 (Year 5) children do during shared writing?

Consider the links made with the children's reading, the teaching strategies and the extent to which the objective (Y5 T1: to analyse the features of a good opening) is achieved.

What equipment do the teachers use to support shared writing?

Make a note of the resources which the teachers use to help the children structure their shared writing.

Figure 8.1 Based on *Literacy Training Pack, Module 4: Shared and Guided Reading and Writing at Pre-Key Stage 1 and Key Stage 1*, p 25

Teaching strategies	Video extract 1	Video extract 2
Encouraging the children to participate.		
Using known texts to generate ideas.		
Discussing audience and purpose.		
Teaching spelling and handwriting.		
Teaching technical vocabulary such as paragraph, sentence, title and heading.		
Refining the sequencing of text, sentence structure and the use of language.		
Teaching layout, sequencing and punctuation.		
Refining writing to clarify its meaning or to improve its impact.		

Task 2: Planning for shared writing

Shared writing should normally be linked with shared reading, which provides themes, structures and ideas from which to work. It could cover some of the same text-, sentence- and word-level objectives as shared reading. Most importantly, it should be written for a purpose: for example, for use as a class poster, leaflet or book, for children in another class (or even another school) or for parents or other adults. It can be displayed on a wall or in a book; it can be hand-written or word-processed.

Choose a fiction text for a particular age group, list the *National Literacy Framework* writing objectives for which it is appropriate and identify the type of writing which could be produced.

Consider the age group for which the text would be suitable and for which term's work it would be most useful. Think about for whom it might be written and its purpose: for example, to retell a story the children have read, to extend or finish a story, and so on (see Wray & Medwell, 1998, 45–46).

● You should now understand the essential characteristics of shared writing, the ways in which it can be linked to shared reading and how to recognise the writing skills which can be taught from texts.

Chapter 9

Guided writing

THEME
Guided writing and its place in the Literacy Hour.

Task 1: The purpose of guided writing and the structure of the session

Guided writing gives children a structure on which to base their independent writing. It provides a focus and a model, since the best way for them to learn to write and to improve their writing is to emulate the best writers. A guided writing session with a small group of children enables the teacher to focus on a particular writing skill and to monitor and assess the children's writing. It also provides the teacher with an opportunity to work with individuals on issues such as editing and planning. Finally, it enables the teacher to be in a position to plan an appropriate activity for the next session. However, if all this is to be done effectively, the groups need to be differentiated according to ability.

The role of the teacher is to provide explicit teaching and feedback.

 In the video extracts (Literacy Training Pack Video 2), what does each teacher of Key Stage 1 and Key Stage 2 children do during guided writing and what do the children learn? Make notes about each teacher.

Consider the way in which each teacher manages his or her group, the focus of the teaching, the way in which the teacher responds to, shares and extends the children's writing and what the children are learning.

 How do the teachers in the video structure their guided writing sessions?

Consider the extent to which the teachers follow the model of guided writing shown in Figure 9.1.

Task 2: Planning guided writing

Both you and the children can enjoy becoming part of a story in various ways. For example:
- by continuing it to reach a conclusion which each of you would prefer to the existing ending;
- giving a greater role to one of the minor characters;
- retelling the story in the children's own words;
- copying the structure of the story, its special textual form or pattern.

Figure 9.1 Observing a guided writing activity

	Teacher	
	Jenny (Year 2)	**Julie (Year 6)**
Genre		
Participation by all the children.		
The level of challenge for the children.		
The specific writing skill which is taught.		
The sentence-level skills which are taught.		
The word-level skills which are taught.		
The extent to which the children construct text, read and re-read it.		

In poetry you can share the fun of substituting some of the words of a poem with others, writing another poem with the same rhythm or making up words in the same way as the poet does.

 By now the Reading Journal of children's fiction which you are required to compile should be well under way; from it select a text which can be used as a starting point for guided writing.

Explain why the text you have chosen is a good model for the children and what kind of writing you would base on it. List the main focus and any other text-level work as well as sentence- and word-level teaching which it supports.

● You should now understand the essential characteristics of guided writing and be able to select texts which are the best models on which children can base their own writing.

Chapter 10

Word-level work

THEMES
The strategies children need to be taught in order to develop their reading and writing skills at word level (phonics, graphic knowledge, analogy and word-recognition), and the terminology used in the word-level strand of the National Literacy Strategy.

Task 1: The terminology

The National Literacy Strategy requires teachers to be familiar with the terminology associated with the text-, sentence- and word-level aspects of reading and writing. The most important terms used in teaching at word-level are onset, rime, phoneme and vowel digraph. Other terms which you will find useful, and which are defined in the glossary of the *Framework for Teaching*, are alliteration, blend, cluster, consonant digraph, diphthong, grapheme and medial phoneme/vowel.

The **onset** of a word is the part which comes before the vowel; the onset of each of the following words is in italics: *m*ap, *ch*eese, *thr*ough, *qu*ick, *kn*ee. In 'quick' the letter 'u' is not counted as a vowel because it is part of the consonant sound 'qu'. In a word which begins with a vowel sound, such as 'out', there is no onset.

The **rime** is the remainder of the word after the onset: m*ap*, ch*eese*, thr*ough*, qu*ick*, kn*ee*. The whole of the word 'out' is the rime.

A **phoneme** is the smallest unit of sound in a word. It is not the same as a letter: for example, there are two phonemes in 'knee' (kn, ee) and three in 'map' (m, a, p), 'cheese' (ch, ee, se), 'through' (th, r, ough), and 'quick' (qu, i, ck). It is generally agreed that there are 44 phonemes in English; you might find it helpful to attempt to list them.

A **vowel digraph** is a combination of two vowels which together produce a phoneme: for example, b *oa* t, st *ea* m, str *ai* ght, st *o* n e (the 'o' and the 'e' combine to produce the long 'o' sound).

Ensure that you can split any word into its onset and rime or its individual phonemes and that you can identify any vowel digraphs within it.

Check your subject knowledge by completing Figures 10.1, 10.2 and 10.3. If you are unsure about any of them, refer to Literacy Training Module 2: Unit 1, *pp 13–18 and* Audio Cassette 1, Side 1 *and* Cassette 2, Side 1.

Figure 10.1 Onset and rime

Word	Onset	Rime
tale		
train		
stripe		
cold		
are		
even		
clue		
shoe		
quack		

Figure 10.2 Phonemes

Word	Phonemes	Number of phonemes	Word	Phonemes	Number of phonemes
rib			through		
too			collection		
speak			television		
door			manage		
scrape			charity		
tight			straight		
is			thumb		
try			thump		
day			elephant		

Figure 10.3 Vowel digraphs (adapted from Literacy Training Pack: Module 2, Unit 1, p 16)

	Rhyming words	Vowel digraphs
they		
wait		
lane		
break		
fail		
be		
chief		
green		
cheap		
sweet		
high		
line		
might		
nice		
slow		
boat		
roll		
slope		

Task 2: Phonics

Teachers have long debated the value of teaching phonics. Some prefer a holistic approach in which children are taught to develop a 'sight-vocabulary' and their knowledge of the correspondence between sounds and symbols emerges from shared reading; others prefer an approach in which there is cumulative learning of the elements of written language: letters and phonemes, then whole words, then phrases and sentences and then texts. Successful reading makes use of a combination of strategies, one of which is phonic knowledge. Graham & Kelly (2000, 82) stress that children need to have a context in which to develop their phonic knowledge; they need to have a purpose for it.

**How can children be taught, in meaningful contexts:
to segment the sounds in words;
to recognise phonemes;
to blend phonemes?**

Watch the sequences 1 – 5 of Module 2 (Literacy Training Pack, Video 1) and make a note of the contexts, strategies and resources used by the teachers to teach these three skills.

Task 3: Word-recognition and analogy

As well as teaching children to split words into segments, to recognise all the different sounds which letters can represent and to blend these sounds to produce words, the teacher needs to ensure that they develop a basic 'sight-vocabulary' of words which do not fit into regular patterns, beginning with those which they will meet most frequently. As they develop their word-recognition skills, children also need to develop a vocabulary of words they understand. As they progress they can be helped to do this by investigating the origins of words.

The use of analogy in reading and spelling is linked to the division of words into onset and rime. Children need to be taught to use analogy: for example, by exchanging onsets and rimes in words such as trick/sick, sack/track, muddle/puddle.

How can you use both a shared and a guided reading session with either Key Stage 1 or Key Stage 2 children to teach word-recognition and, on another occasion, to teach the use of analogy? What independent work could the children carry out and how would you use the plenary session of the Literacy Hour to help them review and consolidate their learning?

Select learning activities for an age group of your choice for each part of the Literacy Hour, bearing in mind that you would not do all of them during the <u>same</u> Literacy Hour. For word-recognition, state the words; and for analogy, the patterns which the children will learn. Make full use of the Activity Resource Sheets and of any other published material which you find helpful (see Appendix 1).

● You should now be familiar with the terminology used in the teaching of reading and writing at word-level. You should also be aware of the phonological knowledge, word-recognition skills and reading strategies (including analogy and segmentation of words) which children need to develop and of some of the ways in which you can teach these.

Chapter 11

Sentence-level work

THEME
Understanding and teaching sentence-level skills.

Task 1: Strategies used in reading

The activity used to introduce teachers to the word-level strand of the *Framework for Teaching* provides a useful focus on all the strategies we use to make sense of text, including the sentence-level skills.

 Identify the processes which you use in order to make sense of text, and highlight those which can be classed as 'sentence-level'.

Read the selected pages of the Literacy Training Pack Module 2, Unit 1 and follow the instructions on the audio cassette. The summary of the activities, on pages 12–13, relates them directly to word-level work: see if you can relate them to a section of the sentence-level work of the Framework for Teaching *for an age group of your choice.*

Task 2: Teaching sentence work

The extract from the radio quiz which you heard at the beginning of the audio cassette (Task 1) illustrated the difficulties which can arise from the use of phonics without a context. The woman who could not combine the syllables of 'potatoes' would have been able to read one word without giving a thought to phonics if she had seen the word in a supermarket display or in a recipe. With regard to words which are *new* to the reader, as highlighted in Task 1, there are several strategies which can be taught to children. Grammar, punctuation and sentence-structure are essential tools in both reading and writing. As they develop their understanding of this, children become less dependent on phonics: for example, a child who reads 'were' for 'wore' in the sentence 'He wore his football kit' can learn to correct this mistake, not only by focusing on the 'or' phoneme, but also by considering the rest of the sentence (and realising that 'were' does not go with 'he', and that in any case a person cannot *be* a football kit!).

 What methods can you use to teach children to use grammar, punctuation and sentence structure in their reading and writing?

Watch Video 2, Module 3: Sequence 3 and make a note of the teaching strategies used and the evidence of children's learning.
Follow Activity 4 (Module 3, pp 19–20), which will focus your attention on an important consideration for sentence structure – the purpose and type of text. Figure 11.1 is a copy of the chart on page 20.

Figure 11.1 (from *Literacy Training Pack Module 2, Teacher's Notes*, page 20)

Text types	Word and sentence features
Recount	
Report	
Explanation	
Instruction	
Exposition (argument or persuasion)	
Narrative	
Poetry	

Watch Video Sequence 6 which shows three examples of investigative work, and sketch a display you could make with children to show how they investigated another aspect of grammar or punctuation. Name a text which would be your starting point and briefly describe the teaching points you would use. Keep a copy of the most useful pages of the text.
Check any basic facts in English Grammar and Teaching Strategies *(Pollock 1999).*

Task 3: Marking children's writing

Marking is not just for assessment purposes. Comments such as 'good', although possibly motivating, do not help the child unless the teacher specifies *what* is good about the writing. It is not helpful if it just makes a judgement. Neither should marking be a correction or proof-reading exercise carried out by the teacher. Marking is one of the ways in which the teacher can help the child to learn. Children's writing, as well as having a purpose, should also have a focus on learning, and the children should know what this focus is: for example, the use of interesting adjectives or powerful verbs, full stops or speech marks.

How can marking be used as a tool for teaching?

Read the Introduction on pages 35–36 of Module 3 and watch Video Sequence 6. Make a note of the ways in which marking is used to foster learning, and then proceed to the individual work on pages 36–37. After this you will find it helpful to read the commentary on pages 38–39.

● You should now understand the ways in which grammar, sentence-structure and punctuation help children to read as well as to write.
● You should be able to plan effective ways in which to teach these sentence-level skills.
● You should know how to use marking as a teaching tool rather than just as a method of assessment.

Chapter 12

Monitoring, assessing and recording reading

THEMES
The methods and purposes of monitoring and assessing children's progress in reading and how these processes can inform teaching.

Task 1: Types and purposes of assessment

Graham & Kelly (2000) describe the four main contexts in which to carry out assessment of children's reading: informal observation, conversations with children, structured semi-formal assessment and formal assessment (including tests and assessment tasks). The last of these is covered in Chapter 27.

Several types of formal assessment are described by Graham & Kelly (*ibid*), who make an important point about summative assessment (the assessment which takes place at the end of a period of teaching): to be of any use it must be informative as well as judgemental. Some standardised reading tests which give children's reading ages, for example, show their overall progress, but indicate neither what they can do nor what specific weaknesses they have.

Wray & Medwell (1998) describe three types of assessment: norm-referenced, diagnostic, and criterion-referenced. Norm-referenced assessment (for example, standardised tests which produce 'reading ages') measures the attainment of a child or group of children against the expected attainment for their age; diagnostic assessment (for example, base-line assessment, which is used to assess children in their first term at school) tests for particular strengths and weaknesses; and criterion-referenced assessment (for example, Statutory Assessment Tasks) measures children's attainment against specified targets (numbered level descriptions).

 Consider the purposes of assessment and the ways in which it can inform the teaching of reading.

Make brief notes about each type of assessment, its purpose and the ways in which it can inform the planning and development of the school curriculum and teachers' planning for reading.

Task 2: Informal assessment by observation and asking questions

Assessment, however informal, is not just a description of what children say or do; it requires judgements to be made. Descriptions should, however, be recorded as evidence of attainment. This evidence helps the teacher to justify to parents, and to authorities such as OFSTED, what he or she teaches – although the purpose of teachers' day-to-day assessment of children's reading, of course, is not only to justify their actions, but to inform their planning.

How do you know that children have learned what you have taught them?
Consider the learning objectives for an English teaching activity which you have planned and make brief notes about the informal observations you can make and the questions you can ask during the course of teaching which will enable you to assess the children's learning. You should always try to find opportunities during your teaching to make such informal assessments of children's learning and to make judgements about their learning in relation to your objectives.

Task 3: Assessing and recording phonemic knowledge

If it is to be managed effectively, formative assessment must be an integral part of teaching. The *Literacy Training Pack* provides an adaptable example which you will find helpful if you can incorporate it into your teaching, but for the purposes of this chapter it is not necessary to *carry out* such an assessment (see Appendices 1–4 of the *Teacher's Notes*).

 Ensure that you are able to carry out an informal assessment of children's phonemic knowledge, record it efficiently and use it to inform what you teach them.

Watch Literacy Training Pack Video 1 *Sequence 3 and read the teacher's record of the assessment. Select one child from the class record and, using the flow chart on page 50 of the Teacher's Notes, identify what you would teach him or her. You do not need to describe how you would teach it.*

Task 4: Miscue analysis

Miscue analysis is assessment in which a child's mistakes are analysed. Many teachers use a simplified form in which mistakes are simply noted and the information kept to form a running record of what the child can do.

The phonemic knowledge assessment procedure in Task 3 assesses phonics only, but miscue analysis helps the teacher to make judgements about every aspect of the child's approach to reading (see Chapters 10 and 11).

 Ensure that you understand miscue analysis and are able to carry it out as one of your school-based tasks.

Make notes on the recommended texts to ensure that you understand the process of miscue analysis and how to carry it out. You will need to copy the miscue analysis sheet (Wray & Medwell, 1998, 169).

Listen to four children of different abilities, each reading a text with which they need some help but which is not so difficult as to cause them frustration (the class teacher can help you with your selection of children and texts). The task will be easier if you tape-record the children reading and carry out the analysis afterwards. Analyse the miscues and make notes about possible teaching strategies.

● You should now be able to monitor and record children's progress in reading. You should be familiar with the different types and purposes of assessment, and be able to assess children's attainment in phonics, carry out miscue analysis and use your assessment of children's attainment to inform your teaching.

Chapter 13

Monitoring, assessing and recording writing

THEMES
The methods and purposes of monitoring and assessing children's progress in writing (excluding handwriting, which is covered in Chapter 15) and how these processes can inform teaching.

Task 1: Finding a common starting point for a class or group

The National Literacy Strategy emphasises that children make better progress in reading and writing when they are taught as a class or in groups rather than as individuals. One factor which affects children's progress is the amount of direct teaching they receive, although this must be combined with purposeful independent work which provides an appropriate level of challenge. When children are taught in groups or as a class they receive more direct teaching overall than when the teacher works with individuals.

For successful class and group teaching there needs to be a common starting point which consolidates the learning of the most able children, extends the learning of the greater part of the class and gives less able children the opportunity to work, with support, at a demanding level. It must also provide challenges for the most able children.

 How can you quickly find an appropriate starting point for a whole-class shared writing activity, or a group guided writing activity?

Read the three samples of children's writing from Key Stage 1 and upper and lower Key Stage 2 children which illustrate the attainment statements derived from the National Literacy Strategy (Literacy Training Pack Module 3, 1998).

During your observation of a class of children, re-read the statements (which are also provided in Figure 13.1) and decide which of them best describe the levels achieved by most of the class. Mark these ✓ or ✗ on Figure 13.1.

From your whole-class assessment, identify what sentence-level work you would teach the class in the next shared or guided writing activity. How would you ensure that all the children were able to work at an appropriate level? (Consider also the independent work which could follow the activity.)

Task 2: Formative assessment

It makes sense to assess children's progress during the course of teaching a particular aspect of writing – if assessment is only carried out at the end of a period of teaching it is then too late to take action to rectify children's weaknesses and to extend their learning. Graham & Kelly (1998) describe how this can be done by sampling.

Figure 13.1 Assessing progress in sentence-level skills (adapted from *Literacy Training Pack, Module 3, Teacher's Notes*, pp 13–15)

End of Key Stage 1	✓ or ✗
Can use grammar implicitly as a cue for prediction and self-correction.	
Can use story and other text structures to support own writing.	
Can recognise and use simple sentence structures (eg writing frames and imitation).	
Can recognise and use full stops and capital letters.	
Years 3 & 4	
Can accomplish consistently all Key Stage 1 tasks.	
Can understand principal word-functions and word-order in sentences, including the identification of parts of speech such as nouns, verbs, adjectives and adverbs.	
Can apply knowledge of parts of speech, word-order and punctuation to improve own writing (eg would be able to re-read work and alter words to strengthen their impact).	
Can understand and use the basic conventions of written standard English (eg accurate use of verb tenses, grammatical agreement and correct use of negatives).	
Can understand, construct and connect simple, compound and increasingly more complex sentences using various connectives.	
Can check for improvement to words, sentences and overall structure and check for accuracy in punctuation (eg can identify where simple but effective alterations improve sense and impact or can identify a muddled sentence in a story and alter it as necessary).	
Years 5 & 6	
Can accomplish consistently all Year 3 and Year 4 tasks.	
Can understand complex sentences and how to construct them from simple ones.	
Can simplify over-complex and sophisticated writing.	
Can understand and use different forms of expression (eg can use a variety of expressions overheard in everyday speech to enliven a dialogue).	
Can check work for appropriateness for purpose, context and audience by considering text type and by improving sentences, words and overall structure (eg can notice when an informal tone has not been maintained and can make the appropriate alterations). Can check for accuracy in punctuation and Standard English.	

Assess a child's writing by sampling it.

Gain the permission of the teacher and child to copy a piece of the child's writing. Make notes on what it shows about his or her attainment in writing in relation to the National Literacy Strategy text-, sentence- and word-level strands. Make notes about the teaching which would help this child.

Task 3: Assessment portfolios

A series of dated and annotated samples of children's writing can provide the teacher with an overview of their progress, with a series of reference points. It can also be shared with the children, by discussing the choice of samples of writing and of their progress. The portfolio can include the children's writing on different subjects.

Teachers usually assess children's attainment in independent writing after they have written the piece, or at least after they have written part of it. It is not feasible to assess during the writing process except during shared or guided writing. Where assessment is carried out after the event, it can be difficult to judge the extent of children's collaboration with others, or the way in which they have used reference sources. Notes about these aspects of the context in which the writing took place should accompany any work which is included in an assessment portfolio.

An assessment portfolio of samples of different children's work from each year group can be used to help a school compare the attainment of different groups. The information provided by this type of portfolio, supported by that from other forms of assessment, can help a headteacher or subject coordinator to pinpoint any strengths or weaknesses which individual teachers have and to provide them with the necessary support and training. It can also help with curriculum evaluation by identifying strengths and weaknesses in different aspects of the children's writing.

With the permission of the child concerned, the class teacher and the headteacher of the school to which you are attached, examine one child's assessment portfolio for English.

Make notes about the child's progress at text-, sentence- and word-level, referring to specific aspects of those strands. You may need to refer also to the National Curriculum, which will have been the main framework for teaching writing before the National Literacy Strategy was introduced.

● You should now be able to assess children's progress in writing against the criteria of the National Curriculum and of the National Literacy Strategy and to use your assessment of children's attainment to inform your teaching.

Chapter 14

Medium- and short-term planning for English

THEMES
Systematic medium- and short-term planning for teaching English using texts as starting points.

Task 1: Medium-term planning

Medium-term planning refers to half-termly planning. It is a process during which the teacher has to address the complex task of selecting an appropriate range of texts at the right levels and linking them to the objectives of the *Framework for Teaching*.

The *Framework for Teaching* provides the long-term planning by identifying, year-by-year and term-by-term, what should be taught at text-, sentence- and word-level. The teacher's professional judgement is needed for medium-term planning of the contexts (the texts from the specified range for each term) in which this work can take place, as well as in organising the class and resources.

 For five weeks' work, select texts across the specified range which are suitable in terms of interest and level of difficulty for a school year of your choice. You could refer back to the texts which you examined during Chapters 4, 5, 6, 8, 9 and 11.

Photocopy the objectives from the Framework for Teaching *for one half-term of the school year you have chosen and make an enlarged copy of the medium-term planner on page 58 of the* Framework. *(The planner has space for eight weeks, but you need only complete five.)*
Enter the names of the texts in the 'Texts' column. Refer to the guidance in Literacy Training Pack Module 1, Teacher's Notes.
Decide which objectives from each strand can be taught together and organise some of them across Week 1; consider those which remain and select some to organise across Week 2.

Task 2: Short-term planning

Short-term planning means weekly planning. The medium-term plan (Task 1) related the objectives of the *Framework for Teaching* to the texts which you chose. The purpose of short-term planning is to specify how those objectives are to be taught within the chosen contexts. This is another part of the planning process which requires the teacher's professional judgement.

With reference to one of the weeks from your medium-term plan, show how you could teach your chosen objectives over the course of a week using the selected texts.

You might find it useful to write this as a lesson plan for the Literacy Hour. Remember that you will need to have at least one learning objective for each part of the hour. Independent activities need a learning objective as well. If you decide to use adult support, include a briefing note in your lesson plan.

● You should now be able to plan the contexts in which to teach the objectives of the National Literacy Strategy over a half-term and to specify how you will teach them over the course of a week.

Chapter 15

Handwriting and the presentation of children's work

THEMES
The ways in which children can learn presentation skills from the texts they read and use these skills to present their own work.

Task 1: From mark-making to handwriting

The *Framework for Teaching* sets out, in the word-level strand, the progression which teachers should follow in teaching handwriting, but this element of the *Framework* is not linked to the notion of children learning by looking at the work of experts. There are many published handwriting schemes which provide models from which the children can learn to write legibly and stylishly (see Appendix 1). Godwin & Perkins (1998, chapter 6) give an account of the development of early writing skills, as do Graham & Kelly (1998, chapter 5), who extend this through Key Stage 1 and Key Stage 2.

 Make sure that you can provide models of handwriting for the children you are teaching.

For many children, the model of handwriting which they see most frequently is that of the teacher. You might need to practise your own handwriting skills so that you can write in the way in which the children are expected to write; look at the recommended published schemes, including computer software.

Task 2: Illustration

What have illustrations to do with writing? Most of us will remember being allowed the privilege, if we finished our writing in time, of drawing a picture to illustrate a story. Slow writers never had the chance to illustrate their writing! The picture would be an 'add-on' at the end of the story; but that is not the way in which most books and other texts are illustrated. If we are teaching children about books we need to teach them how to *use* illustrations, when appropriate, as an integral part of the communication process.

There are several ways in which pictures are important in writing:
- they can help pupils, particularly younger or less able children, with the writing process itself;
- in fiction they often convey information which is not included in the text; many fiction books (for older children and adults as well as for very young children) consist only, or mainly, of pictures;
- illustrations, diagrams and charts in non-fiction are often more important than, or at least as important as, the text;
- illustration is part of the overall presentation of the writing as a creation.

In teaching children to use illustration effectively, consideration must be given to the time which can be devoted to it and at what point illustration can also be a meaningful lesson in art or design technology. The objectives for different subjects can complement one another.

How do illustrations help children to write?

Read Graham & Kelly (1998, 48–50) and examine the illustrated writing of children in Godwin & Perkins (1998) and in the school to which you are attached for observation or teaching practice. Comment on the ways in which illustration assists the process of writing.

How are illustrations used in published texts?

Make notes about the use of illustration in fiction and non-fiction texts. Refer to those which you have included in your Reading Journal (this is an opportunity to add an extra dimension to the Journal).

In the following fiction books illustrations are either part of the story itself or provide insights and information which could not have been conveyed by text alone. Refer to as many of these as possible.

Pre-Key Stage 1 and Key Stage 1
Rosie's Walk *by Pat Hutchins (Puffin, 1970);* Titch *by Pat Hutchins (Puffin, 1971);* Each Peach Pear Plum *by Janet & Allan Ahlberg (Viking, 1978);* Come Away From the Water, Shirley *by John Burningham (Red Fox, 1992);* Once There Were Giants *by Martin Waddell (Red Fox, 1989); and 'lift-the-flap' and 'pop-up' books such as those by Rod Campbell (Macmillan, and also Campbell) and the* Spot *series by Eric Hill (Picture Puffin).*

Key Stage 2
You Should See My Cat *by Martin Oliver (Hippo, 1996);* Mummy Laid an Egg! *by Babette Cole (Red Fox 1993);* Father Christmas Goes on Holiday *by Raymond Briggs (Puffin, 1975) and other picture books by the same author;* War Game *by Michael Foreman (Puffin, 1989); and The* Joke Museum *by Sandy Ransford (Robinson, 1996).*

Task 3: Layout
Children should be encouraged to choose a layout which is appropriate for the purpose, context and audience of their writing. The teacher can encourage them to explore the ways in which published text in a particular genre is set out, for whom it is intended, where it is read, what it is for and how these affect the reader.

Layout includes (depending on the genre): the shape of the text, the standard format for a genre (for example, letters, postcards and poems), columns, boxes, flashes and bubbles, captions, headings, titles, colour and colour-coding, size of text (and variation of size within a text), font (where text is word-processed), position on the page, background, borders, lines, arrows, logos, illustrations and photographs. It includes the physical structure and shape of the book or other medium: for example, poster, notice-board or screen display or scroll. The children can make books of different types: concertina, box, folder or zigzag (see Appendix 1, in particular under **Paul Johnson**).

How does teaching about layout fit into the Literacy Hour and how should it be taught?

On a photocopy of the objectives of the Framework for Teaching, *highlight those from text-level work which indicate progression in learning about layout.*
Look at the objectives for writing in a genre of your choice for any term and describe the way in which you would use a published text to teach children to write and present their own work. Include notes about the ways in which information technology could be used.

● You should now understand progression in handwriting and be able to provide models from which children can learn.
● You should also be aware of the contributions of illustration and layout to texts and understand the approaches which can be used to teach children to investigate them in published texts and to use them in their own writing.

Chapter 16

Spelling

THEME
Ways of teaching spelling strategies at Key Stage 2.

Task 1: The process of spelling

The National Literacy Strategy makes it clear that literate primary pupils should understand the sound and spelling system and use it to read and spell accurately. The aim of word-level work at Key Stage 1 in the National Literacy Strategy is to develop practical reading strategies. This is done by giving children awareness of, and practice in, the common spelling patterns of phonemes, while teaching them the methods they can use to learn how to spell commonly-used words. At Key Stage 2 the work becomes more specific, and is based on investigating spelling patterns and developing rules.

The reasoning behind this philosophy in terms of spelling development can be summarised as:

Stage 1: Speaking and Listening (discriminating sounds);
Stage 2: Spelling (representation of sounds);
Stage 3: Reading (identifying words and building new ones by analogy).

Each term, word work focuses on:

*   identifying sounds and patterns in spoken language;
*   discriminating sounds and patterns in spoken language;
*   recognising spelling patterns of these sounds and words;
*   formulating rules if possible (or exceptions to rules);
*   using phonic cues while reading.

The best way to appreciate the processes which are used in spelling is to examine the ways in which you yourself approach the spelling of difficult words, or words you have never seen written down.

How do you approach the spelling of words you have never seen in written form?

Follow Activity 1 of Literacy Training Pack Module 2, *Unit 3 and make notes about the explanations of the different ways in which the spellings of difficult words might have been tackled. You will need to refer to these notes in Task 3.*

Task 2: The spelling of irregular words

The *Framework for Teaching* provides a list of words which need to be recognised on sight. Most of them are irregular words which children will encounter frequently in everyday reading. It is believed that if they are learned, they will prove vital to later reading success.

How can you teach children how to spell irregular words?

Follow Activities 2 – 4 of the Literacy Training Pack, Module 2, Unit 3 *and collect some ideas of your own with which to complete Figure 16.1. Make use of the published resources for teaching (Appendix 1), the* Activity Resource Sheets *provided with the Module and your observations of teachers at work.*

Complete Figure 16.2 with your own ideas for teaching the irregular words which are listed on it.

Look closely at the ways in which teachers deal with the 'Look (say), Cover, Write (say), Check' strategy: for example, 'Does it look right? Yes? OK to write it down? I'm not sure. Use a dictionary. Check in your spelling list. Now write it out'.

Task 3: Strategies used in spelling

Much of the teaching of spelling at Key Stage 1 will be about the use of phonics (see Chapter 10). But children should also be able to identify analogous spelling patterns in the text: words which begin with the same letter, contain the same letter-string or use the same onset or rime.

At Key Stage 2 children should be given opportunities to investigate words – to understand and formulate rules and their exceptions. The emphasis should be on identifying sounds through spoken language and this exploration should be fun, through playing with predictable and patterned language, poetry, rhymes, tongue-twisters, and so on.

How can teachers help their pupils to develop strategies for spelling which will enable them to progress from a heavy reliance on phonics to an ability to use graphic strategies?

It will help if you can observe and find out about the practical ways in which teachers in the school to which you are attached deal with these spelling issues. You should also make use of published material (see Appendix 1, Teaching resources for the classroom).

● You should now know about the processes which can be used in the spelling of unknown words.
● You should also be able to plan activities for teaching children how to approach the spelling of irregular words, to discover rules (and their exceptions) for spelling and to devise their own rules.

Figure 16.1 Using graphic strategies for the spelling of irregular words (adapted from *Literacy Training Pack, Module 2: Word Level Work, Unit 3*, p9)

- Looking for words within words, for example 'the' in 'they'.
- Grouping words according to spelling pattern, for example: day – away – pay.
- Recognising the tricky part of the word, for example: 'ai' in 'said'.
- Devising mnemonics, for example: 'I am your friEND to the END' (because 'friend' rhymes with 'end'.
- Chanting the letter names in a word and possibly splitting it into syllables, for example: 'P-E-O, P-L-E'.
- Practising writing the word using different media: magnetic letters, sand, letters cut out from paper and so on.
- Using the procedure of 'Look. Read. Cover. Write. Check.'
- Practising the words in short sentences, for example: 'How now brown cow down there!'

Figure 16.2 Strategies for spelling irregular words (from *Literacy Training Pack Module 2: Word-Level Work, Unit 3, Spelling*, p 10)

could
pull
their
what
laugh
don't
brother
many
night
once

Chapter 17

Reading non-fiction

THEMES

The characteristics of different genres of non-fiction text, and how to teach children the process of reading non-fiction.

Task 1: A model for reading non-fiction texts

The National Literacy Strategy proposes an approach to working with non-fiction texts called the 'EXIT' model (EXtending Interactions with Texts). It was developed by the EXEL (Exeter Extending Literacy) project which was based on a series of key ideas which arose from research into the ways in which people interact with non-fiction texts (Wray & Lewis, 1997). The EXEL model for reading non-fiction texts is derived from four main considerations about the process of learning: it is an interaction between what is known and what is to be learned; it is a social process; it is a situated process (firmly based in a context); and it is a metacognitive process (in the most effective learning, learners are aware of their own level of understanding and of how they are achieving it). These terms are explained in more detail by Wray & Lewis (*ibid.*).

The EXIT process consists of ten stages:
1) activating prior knowledge
2) establishing purposes
3) locating information
4) adopting an appropriate strategy
5) interacting with the text
6) monitoring understanding
7) making a record
8) evaluating information
9) assisting memory
10) communicating information.

This unit is about the stages which have particular relevance for reading; Chapter 18 takes up the processes which are more relevant to writing.

How does the EXIT model apply to your own reading of non-fiction texts?

Make notes about the processes which you have used from Stages 1 to 5 of the EXIT model in reading the following non-fiction texts: an instruction manual or a recipe, travel brochures and texts on the reading list for this course (see Appendix 1).

Note any stages which played only a small part, or no part at all, in your reading and consider whether this exercise will alter the way in which you approach your own non-fiction reading.

Task 2: Using the EXIT model

The EXIT model gives three principal ways in which children can be helped to make use of their existing knowledge of a subject before they begin their reading: brainstorming, concept-mapping and the use of 'Know-What-I-Learned' (KWL) grids. The *Literacy Training Pack* and Wray & Lewis (1997) describe them more fully, but do not indicate how these and the other stages of the EXIT model can be used with children who are beginning to read, although David Wray pointed out (Audio Cassette 4) that 'higher-order' and 'advanced' were misleading terms for such reading skills, because very young children, even non-readers, use some of them in everyday situations.

The *Literacy Training Pack* will help you to relate the EXIT model to real teaching situations.

 What can the teacher do to help children of different ages and abilities to approach the reading of non-fiction from the point of view of their existing knowledge and the purposes of their reading?

Read Activities 3 and 4 of Module 6 of the Literacy Training Pack *and carry out Activity 6. Consider what the first and second steps of the EXIT model mean in practical terms at either: Nursery or Reception, Key Stage 1 or Key Stage 2. Select a text for the year group of your choice and plan an activity which will help the children to activate their prior knowledge and establish the purpose of their reading. This activity can be linked with work from another area of the curriculum or, for Nursery/Reception, another of the early learning goals.*

● You should now understand the skills used in reading non-fiction texts.
● You should also be able to use the EXIT model for non-fiction texts to plan reading activities for the Literacy Hour.

Chapter 18

Writing non-fiction

THEMES
The language features and structures of non-fiction genres; skills in writing non-fiction genres.

Task 1: The importance of non-fiction

The National Literacy Strategy maintains that literate primary pupils should, 'understand, use and be able to write a range of non-fiction texts'. This shows the importance now placed upon dealing with, and understanding, the range of non-fiction text types. Work in schools should no longer just be about copying out passages from information texts as 'research', but about helping children to write effectively in a range of information genres.

The text-level objectives in the *Framework for Teaching* are split into 'fiction' and 'non-fiction'. A reason for emphasising specific grammar in the strategy is to enable children to recognise and discuss features of genres – in both reading and writing. The reading and writing of non-fiction should include work at word-, sentence- and text-levels. Each of the 'searchlights' (see Chapter 4) used for reading should also be applied to writing, as the context of children's reading will often provide the context for their writing; the teaching of word- and sentence-level skills will help them to organise their writing and make it accurate.

How much reading and comprehension in the real world is based on fiction?

List everything you have read and written in the past 24 hours. Mark each item 'F' (fiction) and 'N' (non-fiction) and make a note of the reading and writing skills which you used.

Task 2: Writing non-fiction: the EXIT model

At Stage 6 of the EXIT model (see Chapter 17) the reading of a non-fiction text begins to merge with the writing of it. Stage 6 requires children to monitor their own understanding of their reading of a non-fiction text: it is a metacognitive process. The teacher should model the monitoring process during shared and guided reading and writing. A metacognitive chart (Wray & Medwell, 1998, p 165) is particularly useful in helping children to solve the problems they face in their reading of non-fiction.

How do teachers model the process of monitoring the understanding of non-fiction?

Make a note of the strategies used by the teachers shown in Video Sequence 3 (Literacy Training Pack, Module 6, Video 2).

Task 3: Using writing frames

The work of Maureen Lewis and David Wray – in the EXEL project (see Chapter 17) – and the development of writing frames have been central in taking the development of non-fiction forward in schools. The six genres which they identified now appear in the National Literacy Strategy (see Figure 18.1 and DfEE, 1998, *Teacher's Notes*, p 20).

Writing frames provide a simple structure for children's writing. They give them access to the specialist language – for example, of connectives, which make non-fiction writing effective. More importantly, they provide children with a way of responding personally to the text, selecting and thinking about what they have learned, demonstrating their understanding and not just copying out the text. Lewis & Wray (1996) developed a model for teaching non-fiction writing based on Vygotsky's ideas (see Appendix 1) on how children can learn in collaboration with, or by emulating, experts.

You could design some writing frames to deal with the genre you are teaching.
One important issue to consider will be how you help children to move on from using writing frames to becoming independent writers.

What difficulties do children face when writing non-fiction?

List the problems which you have observed when children write non-fiction.

How do writing frames help them to overcome these difficulties?

Watch the video sequence and follow Activity 16 in Module 6 of the Literacy Training Pack.

● **You should now appreciate the problems faced by children writing non-fiction and be able to provide them with the support which they need to overcome these problems, in particular through the use of writing frames.**

Figure 18.1 - Non-fiction text types

Non-fiction text type	Characteristics	Examples and where to find them
Recount		
Procedural (Instructional)		
Report		
Persuasion		
Explanation		
Discussion		

Chapter 19

Note-taking, evaluating information and assisting memory

THEMES
Taking notes on non-fiction texts, identifying bias, fact and opinion in texts and finding ways to remember information.

Task 1: Note-taking

A concern which was expressed about children's reading and writing, at Key Stage 1 in particular, was that it was mainly in fiction genres – stories and rhymes (Wray & Lewis 1997).

At Key Stage 2 children are expected to read a variety of information books about different subjects. These might contain difficult technical terms and explanations of complex processes – often at a higher reading level than their chronological age – and children must sift through the text to select the information which is relevant. This involves reading, discriminating and having enough grasp of written language to be able to put such information into their own words – a different language.

The National Curriculum requires children to be taught skills such as skimming and scanning, finding information, posing pertinent questions, identifying the precise information they wish to know, making succinct notes and re-presenting information in different forms. This requirement assumes that children are reading for understanding – not simply decoding.

The *Framework for Teaching* requires that notes are taken – see the Writing Composition sections – but does not offer any real strategies.

 What practical activities can you plan for shared and guided reading and writing of non-fiction texts which will help children to take notes effectively?

For an age group and topic of your choice (linked to another subject) and using information books of your choice, make notes about the ways in which you would use both shared reading and guided reading to teach children how to take notes. Do not try to teach too many strategies at once; select those which are the best for the purpose.

The texts on the reading list will help you to be aware of the process of note-taking and provide some practical ideas which you can adapt. Figure 19.1 provides some ideas suggested by teachers.

Figure 19.1 Teachers' suggestions to show children that 'notes' do not mean 'scribbles', but that notes should be organised and tidy.

Encourage the children to read with a specific purpose in mind: to ask questions.

Present information in another form: for example, draw a labelled diagram from a piece of text using key words.

Extract information and write it on a chart.

Identify and remember the important points in a passage that has been copied: underline the key points.

Underline different aspects in a copied passage by using different colours.

Put the information in chronological order: some information will come from non-chronological texts but the information may have to presented chronologically.

Use a non-linear method: make web diagrams.

Use abbreviations: for example, e.g.; i.e.

Figure 19.2 (from Mee, Arthur [undated, probably 1940s] *The Children's Encyclopedia*, Educational Publishing Company)

In his boat, with mat sails, he made dangerous voyages from time to time, thousands of natives bidding him farewell with songs of sorrow. Six times Williams was nearly drowned, the sea waves dashing his vessel on the rocks. He was spared, however, to evangelise these South Sea Islands, and translated the New Testament into Raratongan. He came home after many years to plead the cause of the natives in England, and, returning in 1839, he landed with three companions on the shore at Erromanga. But the natives there were hostile. A big savage struck Williams on the head, killing him, and a shower of arrows followed. In a few moments the rippling water was red with the blood of the noblest man that has ever gone to those far-off isles in the South Sea laden with blessings for the ignorant and the outcast.

Task 2: Evaluating texts

Wray & Lewis (1997) argue that all texts are biased because the writer's views influence his or her choice of words; they support this assertion with some compelling examples from newspapers, and note the importance of recognising bias in text because of the unconscious ways in which it can influence the reader's opinions. Texts such as the one shown in Figure 19.2 would not be allowed in school libraries today; and Wray & Lewis (*ibid.*) point out that adults influence children by this censorship of texts.

How can you help children to separate bias, opinion and fact in texts?

Read Figure 19.2 and complete the column headed 'fact' in Figure 19.3. Think about the way in which the writer described the facts and complete the column headed 'opinion'. Try to match each opinion with a fact. What does the passage tell you about the writer's views of the indigenous people of Erromanga, their culture and beliefs? Compare these with the facts.

Task 3: Assisting memory

Children, like adults, forget most of what they have read. How can we help them (and ourselves) to remember the important points from their/our reading? The processes of note-taking and evaluating (separating fact from opinion), as covered in Tasks 1 and 2, provide a structure which assists memory, as does the presentation of the information for someone else (Chapter 18). These processes make the reader *interact* with the text rather than absorb information passively.

Another process which helps with presentation and writing is that of restructuring text. This can be done in several ways: for example, making grids, comparison charts, 'fact trees'/'fact wheels', lists, maps, diagrams, annotated pictures, Venn diagrams, flow charts, fact files, quizzes and board games; and labelling and genre exchange, such as converting a radio or television script into a newspaper report (Wray & Lewis, *ibid.*). The restructuring of text can be described as 'an advanced reading skill' but that does not mean that it is only for Key Stage 2. Children in Years 1 and 2 can rearrange information in many of the forms listed. Some reading schemes provide very useful photocopiable activity sheets which give a structure for this (see Moorcroft 1997a, 1997b).

Select a non-fiction text and explain how you can assist your own memory of it.

Use as many of the suggested devices for assisting memory as are appropriate. Treat the text in ways in which you would expect children of an age group of your choice to treat it (although they might not use <u>all</u> these devices).

● You should now be able to show children how to take purposeful, well-organised notes.
● You should be able to show them how to recognise fact, opinion and bias in a text.
● You should also be able to model techniques of using information in ways which help the children to remember it.

Figure 19.3 Fact, opinion and bias

Fact	Opinion

Chapter 20

Speaking and listening

THEME
The contribution of discussion to children's learning in English.

Task 1: The place of speaking and listening in the teaching of English

The recorded interviews (*Literacy Training Pack, Video 1* and *Audio Cassette 1*) with the authors of the *Framework for Teaching* indicated that the concept of a Literacy Hour arose from the suggested time allocation for *English in the National Curriculum* (the Dearing Report, 1995) – five hours. Five hours could easily be implemented as one hour per day and this, they said, meant that teachers would spend no more time on English than they had before.

This assertion does not take into account the differences in content between *English in the National Curriculum* and the *Framework for Teaching*. The former comprised three attainment targets – Speaking and Listening, Reading, and Writing – while the latter focuses on reading and writing within the three strands of word-, sentence- and text-level work. The Literacy Hour is organised in a way which requires discussion between teacher and children (during guided and shared reading and writing) and among the children (during independent work), but none of the objectives of the *Framework* contains a clear focus on the progression of skills in oracy.

How can teachers solve the problem of teaching the very prescriptive Literacy Hour, yet cover the National Curriculum (which is still a statutory requirement), on whose attainment targets children are assessed?

Photocopy Attainment Target 1 (Speaking and Listening) for Key Stages 1 and 2 from the National Curriculum for English. *On the photocopy, highlight the objectives which also appear (sometimes in different words) in the* Framework for Teaching.

Consider the objectives which you have not highlighted. You should find that most of them are concerned with the teaching of speaking and listening for its own sake (to develop children's skills in oracy) rather than as a tool for the development of skills in literacy.

You will need your highlighted photocopy for Task 2.

Task 2: Speaking and listening as tools for learning

Grugeon *et al.* (1998, chapter 1) emphasise the difference between discussions among children *with* and *without* an adult present. One tape-recording which is transcribed in this chapter compares the discussion of a group of children (about their observations of snails) without an adult present, and their discussion with the teacher; another shows the level of learning of four boys discussing a poem.

How can the teacher encourage purposeful pupil-pupil talk which develops skills in both oracy and literacy during the Literacy Hour in Key Stages 1 or 2, or during teaching and learning activities which take place in the Nursery?

Describe an activity for children of an age group of your choice which encourages pupil-pupil and pupil-teacher/teacher-pupil talk and list some of the questions which you would ask the children. Specify learning objectives in oracy and literacy and how you will know the extent to which they have been attained.

Task 3: Learning about talk, with particular reference to story-telling

As with text of different genres, the children can learn about the talk of different genres by listening to experts: interviewers, presenters, actors, television and radio journalists and news-readers, entertainers and story-tellers. The teacher can draw the children's attention to the characteristic features of each kind of talk: the 'person' in which it is spoken, the 'voice' (active or passive), the type of language (personal or impersonal, formal or informal), the tense, the use of dialect words and contractions, the length and complexity of sentences and the use of dialogue.

When a story is told, the author has to consider the needs of the audience in a different way from when it is read, because the context and purpose are different. These differences can be discussed: for example, a story for younger children can contain words they understand but cannot read, and the reader can use his or her voice to create an impression or mood.

Turn to pages 44 – 67 of the Curriculum Guidance for the Foundation Stage. *Read and make notes on this crucial stage of children's development. You may find several examples of what under-fives can do, which older children may not be able to do. How can we help the weak speaker at KS 1/2? Use the QCA guidance on Teaching Speaking and Listening to help you.*

● You should now be aware of the ways in which you can encourage discussion among children which furthers their learning in English and across the curriculum.
● You should be aware of the ways in which children's skills in oracy can contribute to literacy.
● You should be able to plan activities which teach children about the genre of storytelling.

Chapter 21

Poetry

THEME
Teaching poetry in the primary classroom.

Task 1: Your attitude towards poetry

We can all remember being faced with a blank sheet of paper in school and asked to 'write a poem' about something – a daunting task for an adult, never mind a child. This approach to poetry in school arises from the classical idea of a hierarchy of literature, where poetry is seen as being very near the top of our cultural tradition. Often poetry was taught in schools only because it was 'poetry' – the highest of the written arts.

The Bullock Report of 1975 (see Appendix 1) noted that out of 1000 post-16 exam students of English literature only 170 said they would read any poetry again. Another report on middle schools (Middle Schools Survey, 1983, see Appendix 1) said: 'Frequently … poetry was used by teachers only as a source of material for comprehension exercises and for handwriting practice; for some children their only contact with poetry was through course books.'

As Orme (1992) notes, young children enjoy reading and writing poems. So what happens at school? Poetry in the form of the ballad was one of the earliest forms of story telling – a method of communicating narrative orally to an illiterate population. The rhythm and the rhyme made the verse easy to remember.

 Think back to the last time you wrote a poem. Did you find it difficult? Have you written one since you left school? Why should you?

Jot down some memories of the kinds of things you did when studying poetry at school. Did you enjoy it? Why/why not? Why do you think you were doing this kind of work?

Consider your notes about your own experience in relation to the ideas of the authors in the reading list (Appendices 1 and 2).

Task 2: Reading and writing poetry

The *Framework for Teaching* encourages teachers to read all kinds of poetry and verse with children, including playground chants, nursery rhymes, action rhymes, advertisements and jingles as well as more formal poetry (Figure 21.1). The text-level objectives include teaching *about* poetry – different types of poetry, the devices used by poets, the 'messages' of poems and even the shapes of poems. There are also word-level objectives which can be taught through poetry (Grugeon *et al.*, 1998): the use of rhyme to teach about phonics and onset and rime, and of rhythm to teach about syllables. Grugeon *et al.* (*ibid.*) refer to research which indicates the connection between children's ability to appreciate rhyme and rhythm and their ability to read and spell.

Figure 21.1 Poetic forms and devices

Poetic form	Example of a poem (including the author, anthology, publisher and date)	Poetic devices used
Ballads		
Calligrams		
Cinquains		
Concrete or shape poems		
Couplets		
Elegies		
Epitaphs		
Free verse		
Haikus		
Humorous poems		
Hymns		
Limericks		
Monologues		
Narrative poetry		
Nonsense verse		
Raps		
Rhyming poems		
Songs		
Tankas		

It is important, however, that teachers do not lose sight of the fun of poetry – the 'playing with words' of poets like Roger McGough and the clever use of humour by poets like Charles Causley and E V Rieu. In poetry, children can ignore the rules of grammar and put words together in new ways.

Within the *Framework for Teaching*, how can you <u>enjoy</u> poetry with children?

For a year group from each stage of primary education (Nursery/Reception, Key Stage 1 and Key Stage 2) choose two poems which you would enjoy reading with the children: one which has immediate 'fun' appeal, and another which can be just as enjoyable (possibly because of the message it conveys or the story it tells). Consider the questions which you would ask and the instructions you would give for group discussion to help the children to explain what they like about the poems, and to help them to build up their own understanding and appreciation of them.

Task 3: Appreciating and using the technical features of poetry

The *Framework for Teaching* requires teachers to understand and teach many technical terms used in poetry, about the different forms of poetry, and about the devices used by poets. As with other kinds of writing, children can learn from experts. The teacher's role is to help the children to recognise a particular form of poetry and to provide a structure which can help them to write in a similar form. They should also be given help to identify and practise the devices used by poets so that they can use them in their own poems.

What can you teach children <u>about</u> poetry?

Either
Make a note of all the Framework's text-level objectives about reading and writing poetry and make sure that you know what all the technical language means (the different forms of poetry and the devices used by poets). Look for examples of each form of poem and identify the devices used by the poet. Figure 21.1 provides a structure for this.

Or
Describe how you would use poetry in a nursery or reception class to encourage literacy.

● You should now appreciate the different forms of poetry and the devices used by poets and be able to plan activities in which children learn to appreciate and to write different forms of poetry.

Chapter 22

Drama

THEME
The contribution of drama to children's learning in English.

Task 1: The place of drama in the teaching of English

The National Curriculum contains numerous references, in all three attainment targets for English, to the requirement for teaching drama linked to oracy and literacy across different genres (see Clipson-Boyles, 1998). Although the objectives of the *Framework for Teaching* concern literacy, there are also opportunities for developing oracy (see Chapter 20), which is an important part of drama. But drama can contribute to learning in ways other than as a vehicle for teaching oracy. It can help children to learn about the critical features of both fiction and non-fiction texts: for example, when they play in the 'role-play' corner, work 'in role' (of a character in a story), act out conversations between real or imaginary people or enact and then report arguments.

 Identify the objectives of the *Framework for Teaching* which can be taught through drama.

> *In your planning for teaching literacy in a way which includes drama and oracy, you will find it helpful to keep a separate file for some of your work from this and Chapter 20.*

> *Figure 22.1 will help you to record your responses for this task.*

Task 2: Using drama to develop literacy skills

Many of the drama methods described by Clipson-Boyles (1998) can be incorporated into the Literacy Hour for text-level fiction and non-fiction work in several different genres. They can also form part of the teaching of other subjects such as history, science and design technology. These cross-curricular links mean that skills in literacy can enrich the children's learning in other subjects.

 How can the teacher include drama in the Literacy Hour at Key Stages 1 and 2, and use role-play in the Nursery, to develop children's literacy skills?

> *For children of a year group and term of your choice, describe an activity in which drama (other than play-scripts) is used, first in a fiction genre, and then in a non-fiction genre. Identify the objectives from the* Framework for Teaching *towards which these activities work.*

> *Describe the ways in which you would set up a role-play area in a Reception class or Nursery for a topic of your choice, and the opportunities it would provide for the children's role-play.*

Figure 22.1 The use of drama for teaching literacy

Year and Term	Objective number and description
Reception	
Year 1	
Term 1	
Term 2	
Term 3	
Year 2	
Term 1	
Term 2	
Term 3	
Year 3	
Term 1	
Term 2	
Term 3	
Year 4	
Term 1	
Term 2	
Term 3	
Year 5	
Term 1	
Term 2	
Term 3	
Year 6	
Term 1	
Term 2	
Term 3	

Task 3: Teaching drama as a creative art

As you will have noticed, drama can be planned in conjunction with any subject, so the possibilities which are discussed in this task are connected with English outside the Literacy Hour, but based on texts which the children read *in* the Literacy Hour and, possibly, in connection with research for other subjects. The principal objectives are concerned with developing an understanding of drama as an art form, but there are also objectives which link to literacy, since the types of activity suggested require the children to read and discuss a text in great detail in order to present all, or part, of it in a dramatic form.

Having read Clipson-Boyles (1998) select, for a year group of your choice, a text which the children can enact as a mime or tableau. How would you prepare a group of children with little experience of drama to carry out the activity?

Tableau and mime have been suggested because they are performed without words; this means that the children have to develop a very good understanding of the text. They cannot rely on their skills in converting a dialogue to a play-script (letting the words do the work); nor can they rely on their reading skills – using the expression suggested by the sentence structure, punctuation and devices such as italics for emphasis. They have to read the text very carefully, discuss it and decide on the ways in which the characters move, their postures and their facial expressions. They also have to think about their positions on the 'stage' and the timing of their movements. Careful consideration of these aspects will enrich the ways in which they enact plays with spoken words on other occasions.

● You should now be able to identify opportunities for introducing drama into English and into other subjects, and to plan learning activities which use drama to develop children's oracy and literacy.
● You should be able to plan learning activities which teach drama as a creative art in its own right.

Chapter 23

Working with parents and other adults

THEMES
Harnessing the potential of parents and other adults to enrich children's learning in English. Organising the work of other adults in the classroom.

Task 1: The value of parents' contributions to children's learning

A summary of two significant pieces of research into children's use of language at home is provided by Godwin & Perkins (1998), both of which demonstrate the extent to which parents' contributions to their children's learning are underestimated.

Godwin & Perkins (*ibid.*) discuss the ways in which children in their early years learn at home about language. They note that when children are with their families they are exposed to spoken and written language in different contexts, and that they have opportunities to speak, listen, read and write for recognisable purposes; they describe some of the possibilities of encouraging this source of learning.

Graham & Kelly (2000) caution against underestimating the contributions of parents to children's learning, not just in the early years but throughout the primary school. They quote research which indicates that children's progress in reading is better when parents work in partnership with the school.

 How do parents help their children to develop skills in oracy and literacy?

Summarise your reading and make notes about your observations of children interacting with their parents or carers in public places. Notice the ways in which the adults help the children to learn and the learning which takes place.

Task 2: Partnership with parents to develop literacy

Partnership between parents, children and teachers (PACT) to promote literacy refers mainly to the work which the parents and children do together at home, but it can include parental involvement in school (see Task 3). Godwin & Perkins (1998) discuss partnership with the parents of children in their early years, and Graham & Kelly (2000) extend this to take in the whole of primary education; Graham & Kelly (1998) also point out the value of the writing which children do at home and suggest ways in which it can be brought into school.

The above sources also emphasise the importance of partnership with parents of children for whom English is an additional language or of those with special educational needs; these are covered in Chapters 24 and 25 respectively.

How do schools create partnerships with parents to promote literacy?

List the ways in which schools can plan for partnership with parents to promote literacy and find out how the school to which you are attached involves parents in their children's learning in English. Ask for copies of any information which the school provides for parents about reading and writing, and note the ways in which the school encourages parents to help and the advice which it provides for them. Also note the ways in which the school learns from the parents about their children.

Task 3: Parents and other adults in the classroom

Before the late 1980s it was rare to find adults other than teachers in classrooms except for non-teaching assistants in Nursery and Reception classes, and care assistants to help children with special educational needs. Many schools now have rotas of both paid and unpaid helpers in classrooms. Godwin & Perkins (1998) describe the possible roles of such helpers and the ways in which teachers need to plan their work with them. The authors make specific references to Nursery and Reception classes, but what they say is relevant to the deployment of parents and other helpers in teaching children of any age.

Other adults can be invaluable in the management of the Literacy Hour as they can work with groups of children who need support while the teacher is engaged with guided reading or guided writing with another group. Their help enables groups to get started on activities which they can continue on their own. They must not provide so much support that the children lose opportunities to become independent learners, but they can assist the children to do this: for example, by helping them to use dictionaries and other reference material and by directing them to other independent learning strategies.

How can the teacher make the best use of the help of other adults in the classroom?

Notice how the school to which you are attached uses the help of additional adults and make notes about the ways in which their work is organised. Note too how the teachers ensure that these helpers provide the right kind of help for the children, and check that they understand the purpose of what they are doing.

● You should now appreciate the contribution which parents and other adults can make to children's learning in English.
● You should also know how to plan and organise the assistance of other adults in the classroom.

Chapter 24

English as an additional language (EAL)

THEME
Teaching children whose home and community language is not English.

Task 1: The needs of children whose home language is not English

Schools are required to make provision for pupils for whom English is an additional language, as outlined in the National Curriculum (English), and SCAA (1996) provides a set of key principles for addressing the needs of those pupils. *Curriculum Guidance for the Foundation Stage* provides support for under-fives.

It is important to avoid stereotyping; children for whom English is an additional language have a variety of experiences and home circumstances in both oral and written language, as noted by Clipson-Boyles (1998, p 77).

Teachers need to find out about their pupils' individual circumstances; Clipson-Boyles (*ibid.*) describes some of the ways in which they can do this, and Graham & Kelly (1998) point out the need to know about the ways in which people learn language, in particular a second or subsequent language.

 How can teachers find out about the experience of spoken and written language (both in English and in the home and community language) of children for whom English is an additional language?

Summarise your reading and make notes about the experiences which children for whom English is an additional language might have of spoken and written English and of their home and community language. Find out about the experiences of these children in the school to which you are attached, if there are any; if there are not, you should check with other students.

Task 2: Teaching children for whom English is an additional language

Researchers in EAL stress the importance of giving a high status to the children's home and community languages. The ways to do this include: the encouragement of the children's oral and written use of these languages and their sharing of them (and their differing cultural experiences) with others in the class; the provision of dual-language texts and texts written in the home and community languages only; partnership with the children's families. This work can also enrich the social, spiritual and cultural experiences of the class. A word of caution: if you do not speak the community languages you will need to check the meanings of any texts you display to avoid causing offence, for example by the inappropriate display of religious texts.

Dual-language texts can be used for re-telling stories in both languages, improvising alternative endings for a story and making use of drama (Grugeon *et al*, 1998 and Clipson-Boyles, 1998).

Teachers need to organise such things as the provision of opportunities for these children to work with others who speak their own language, English only and other languages; they also need to organise the help of support teachers who speak the children's home and community language, and of interpreters (who might be members of the children's families, or other people from the local community).

 How can teachers ensure that they are providing the best possible learning experiences for children for whom English is a second language?

In addition to your reading, find out about the policy and practice for EAL of the school to which you are attached. Make notes about the ways in which teachers show respect for the children's home and community languages and encourage them to speak, read and write in both English and these languages.

Task 3: Resources

Dual-language books are obvious resources, but these should be selected with care (*see* Graham & Kelly, 1998). Other resources include puppets and drama props and other provision for role-play (Grugeon *et al.*, 1998 and Clipson-Boyles, 1998). Tape-recordings of books in English, in other community languages and in two languages can also be useful.

The children can make their own resources, such as books, puppets and masks. They could also bring into school artefacts from home connected with cultural events which are important in their home and community.

A very valuable resource is the expertise of the children's parents, other members of their families and other adults who speak their community language; in addition to supporting the children in the classroom, they can help them to share their language and culture with the rest of the class.

 Add to your Reading Journal details of dual-language books and other texts, and of those written in the languages of other communities.

It is difficult for someone who does not speak the other language to judge the quality of the text (or of the translation), so teachers need to seek the help of EAL specialists. Sources of useful texts include shops in areas where there are people from different ethnic backgrounds, as well as places of worship such as mosques, synagogues, gurdwaras and Hindu and Buddhist temples.

● You should now appreciate the variety of experiences and needs of children for whom English is an additional language.
● You should also be able to plan for these children appropriate learning experiences which value their home and community language.

Chapter 25

Special educational needs (SEN)

THEME
Teaching children with special educational needs in English.

Task 1: From assessment to individual education plans

Schools are required to follow the *Code of Practice* (DfE, 1994) with regard to pupils with special educational needs. Such pupils are identified either by routine assessment or by specific assessment which is carried out because of the concerns of their teachers or parents. The *Code of Practice* requires schools to grade these pupils from 1 to 5, according to the level of their need, and to keep a special educational needs register. Some pupils on this register will need the help of specialists such as speech therapists and language support teachers but, if their need is deemed great enough, their teachers will work with the school's special educational needs coordinator (SENCO) and external specialists to compile an individual education plan (IEP) for them. The IEP is based on a detailed assessment of the pupil; it contains targets for attainment in finely-graded steps which allow even small achievements to be recorded. Many pupils on the register will not require an IEP, but they might need specific teaching in some aspects of their work and/or extra support in the classroom.

The SENCO is responsible for arranging reviews of the progress of pupils on the SEN register. These reviews are carried out at regular intervals and include contact with the child's parents. As a result of the review, changes might be made to the IEP, or the child might be taken off the SEN register.

 Ensure that you know the requirements for schools with regard to SEN in general. Then find out how schools identify pupils with special educational needs in English and how they assess these needs.

Read the SEN policy, and other guidelines for SEN, of the school to which you are attached and, if possible, find out how the SENCO organises assessment, reviews of pupils' progress, contact with their parents and the preparation of IEPs. Find out also about the external specialists available to support these children in their learning in English.

Task 2: Teaching children with special educational needs in English

Graham & Kelly (2000) describe the kinds of teaching which can help children who are experiencing difficulties with reading, but what they say is also relevant for those who have difficulties with writing. They emphasise the need to work on the self-esteem of these children, who have experienced failure and may suffer from lack of confidence.

Few teachers have full-time support for pupils with special educational needs. They need to provide differentiated activities for them, based on their IEPs if they have them, and at other times include them in whole-class work such as shared reading or shared writing. Many schools enlist support teachers and non-teaching assistants (including volunteers such as parents) to help those children for part of the time. This help can take many forms (Graham & Kelly, *ibid.*) and can be provided by an assistant *in* the classroom, by taking the children *out* of the classroom for individual or group work, or even by arranging for them to work with specialists in language centres.

 How can teachers ensure that they are providing the best possible learning experiences in English for children with special educational needs?

In addition to your reading, find out how the school to which you are attached uses assessment, and how the resulting IEPs are used to inform the learning experiences which are provided for children with special educational needs. Notice the ways in which teachers foster the children's self-esteem.

Task 3: Resources

Some reading schemes have supplementary material to help children who have difficulties with reading; others are written specifically *for* those children. The latter have subject matter which is likely to interest older children with special educational needs, although they have text at the level of books for younger children.

Books with illustrations are particularly helpful for children who are struggling with their reading, provided that the illustrations and context are not 'babyish' or demeaning. Examples of useful books include *Fred* (Posy Simmonds, Cape), *Tusk, Tusk* (David McKee, Andersen), the *Dr Xargle* books (Jeanne Willis and Tony Ross, Red Fox) and *Father Christmas* (Raymond Briggs, Puffin). But do not ignore other genres of text which might mean a lot to the children themselves: for example, when one SEN teacher asked her group to bring their favourite books to school, one child brought the *Argos* catalogue! He could read special offers which were written in text at a level far above the rest of his reading.

 Add to your Reading Journal details of books and other texts which can be used for teaching children with special educational needs in reading and writing.

Make notes about the content and reading level of the texts, the ways in which illustrations are used and the age range for which they are suitable.

● You should now have an understanding of the ways in which the attainment of children with special educational needs in English can be assessed, and how their needs can be met.
● You should know how to plan (with the support of specialists where appropriate) learning experiences which will help children with special educational needs to make the best possible progress in English.

Chapter 26

The needs of very able children

THEME
Teaching children whose ability in English is well above average.

Task 1: The opportunities offered by the *Framework for Teaching*

The drive behind the National Literacy Strategy (as noted in Chapter 3) was not only to even out variation in attainment in literacy but also to tackle the low levels of attainment in literacy in many schools. This emphasis on raising the lower standards was made explicit by the Secretary of State for Education, David Blunkett, in his Foreword to the *Framework for Teaching*. Less emphasis has accordingly been placed on developing the skills of the most able children.

Wray & Lewis (1997) summarise the findings of some of the surveys of children's standards of literacy which were carried out between 1978 and 1995. The evidence suggested that few children at Key Stage 2 were being taught advanced reading and writing skills (the skills beyond knowing how to read and write, including many of the text-level objectives for Key Stage 2 in the *Framework for Teaching*).

Some of the research to which Wray & Lewis refer indicates that one of the problems faced by teachers was their lack of understanding of what 'advanced skills' were and how they were to be developed, and OFSTED (1995) expressed concerns about the subject knowledge and understanding of many teachers.

The *Framework for Teaching* has addressed these problems by providing a structure for the development of children's skills in reading and writing and describing what these skills are. The *Literacy Training Pack* helps teachers to improve their own subject knowledge. It suggests ways in which teachers can differentiate whole-class shared reading and writing to enable children of different abilities to take part at appropriate levels of challenge. It also shows how teachers can plan and teach guided and independent reading and writing activities for children grouped by ability.

 During the Literacy Hour, how can teachers cater for very able children?

Watch the suggested sequences of Modules 4 and 5 of Video 2 and make notes about the teaching of very able children. Take particular note of the ways in which the teachers have organised their classes and the questions they use in both whole-class and group situations.

Task 2: Developing your own skills in teaching very able children

To teach *any* children you need first to find out what they already know and can do. You should refer to the records of their attainment, and you can assess them informally on the topic you are going to teach: plan an activity which begins at a common level for the whole class or group, and then assess their knowledge, understanding and skills through discussion. The case-studies in Wray & Medwell (1998) indicate how this can be done and how it can provide real challenges for children.

How can you adapt your lessons so that they challenge the very able children?

Choose a lesson which you taught during teaching practice and consider how well it met the needs of the very able children. Bear in mind how easily they answered questions and completed their tasks, what they already knew and what they learned, and how motivating they found the work. Think of ways in which you could have altered the lesson to take these children further.

Task 3: 'Gifted' children

Every class has children of above-average ability, but you might be lucky enough to teach a child of exceptional ability. You might not immediately recognise such gifts – you might even think that he or she is of below average ability. One of the signs is an extremely keen interest in a particular topic, a desire to find out about only that topic, and probably a very high level of knowledge and understanding of it. You are trying to teach the Literacy Hour – but all he or she wants to do is to talk about space, or birds, or architecture, or whatever.

If you talk to the child about this special interest you might be astonished to find that he or she knows far more about it than you do. So what do you do? You could ask the child to prepare a presentation about the subject for the rest of the class (the presentation can be composed during the Literacy Hour); you could provide independent reading and writing activities based on texts of different genres about the subject.

These children have special educational needs of a different kind; there is no statutory requirement to provide IEPs for them, but if you can rise to the challenge, you will be meeting their needs – and you will find it immensely rewarding!

What kinds of guided and independent reading and writing activities would you plan for a child who achieves very little during the Literacy Hour but whose avid reading about horses, for instance, reveals a very high level of ability?

Look for different genres of text about the subject and think of ways in which it can be incorporated into the Literacy Hour. Add the details of these texts to your Reading Journal. Remember, you might have to do this kind of thing during your teaching career.

● You should now know how to plan differentiated learning experiences in which the whole class can work together and others in which groups of children can work separately.
● You should also know how to go about setting appropriate tasks for children of high ability in English and have some ideas on how to meet the challenge of 'gifted' children.

Chapter 27

Statutory assessment

THEMES
National expectations of children's ability at age five, and statutory assessment at the ends of Key Stages 1 and 2

Task 1: Assessment of children under the age of five

There are national standards for children at the age of five described as *Early Learning Goals*. Nursery and Reception teachers can monitor the progress of their pupils towards more goals by carrying out baseline assessment (the assessment of children during their first term at school). The criteria against which assessments are made are grouped into six main areas of learning, one of which is communication, language and literacy. These statements about children's attainment based on its criteria can be related to Level 1 of the National Curriculum.

As noted by Godwin & Perkins (1998), the learning outcomes described by any government agency need to be interpreted by the teacher and translated into descriptions of observable behaviour in order to be meaningful.

What do the early learning goals for communication, language and literacy mean in terms of observable behaviour, and by what methods can baseline assessment be carried out?

Describe the context in which you could carry out baseline assessment in an aspect of your choice of language and literacy. If children fulfil a criterion, what would you expect them to be able to do? What would you look for? How would you assess their progress by the end of the Reception year in this aspect of language and literacy?

Task 2: Standard Assessment Tasks (SATs) at the end of Key Stage 1

Statutory assessment provides information which enables national standards to be monitored. It also enables local authorities to monitor the standards of their schools, and schools to gain an overview of the attainment and progress of their pupils. The assessment of children at the end of Key Stage 1 in English covers reading and writing. Their attainment is judged against the criteria of level descriptions provided in the National Curriculum (see Chapters 12 and 13). National expectations are that children should reach Level 2 (Level 2 is now the norm for seven-year-olds, which means that what was intended as criterion-referenced assessment has become norm-referenced).

The teacher makes the initial judgement of the child's level of ability and (for the reading test) selects an appropriate book from a given list (the book should not be familiar to the child - i.e. it should not have been in the class library or used for shared or guided reading). Children who are judged to be at Level 1 do a different test from the others, but if they perform well on this they can do the Level 2 test. Children who do well on the Level 2 test can take the Level 3 test. For writing, the children do a writing task related to other work in the classroom. There is a formal spelling test for children judged to be attaining Level 2 or above.

How can teachers ensure that children have equal opportunities in SATs?

Describe the factors which could affect a child's performance in a reading, writing or spelling test, and note the ways in which teachers can prepare children for statutory assessment.

Task 3: SATs at the end of Key Stage 2

Children are expected to reach Level 4 at the end of Key Stage 2. At Key Stage 2, as at Key Stage 1, teachers must make the initial judgement of children's levels of ability to decide which tests they do, and the appropriate books for the reading test. Children who are at Levels 1 and 2 read with the teacher, following the same procedure as children at the end of Key Stage 1, but using different books. The others take the combined reading and writing tests, and any who are thought to be working at Level 6 do an extension paper. In addition to the reading and writing tests there is a separate spelling and handwriting test. With this, too, there is an extension test for children who are thought to be working at Level 6.

How is teacher assessment used to support judgements about children's attainment at the end of Key Stage 2?

From three Year 6 children, collect six samples of writing in different genres and assign a level to each piece with reference to the National Curriculum. Refer to QCA (1999b) and any copies of recent assessment booklets which are available.

● You should now be familiar with the methods of statutory assessment in English, and know how to mark these asessments and record the marks.
● You should also know about the requirements for schools to report pupils' levels of attainment.

Appendix 1: Further reading

General background reading

1996 *Oxford Reading Tree Rhyme and Analogy Teacher's Book* Oxford University Press
Barnes *et al*. 1971 *Language, the Learner and the School* Penguin
Beard, R (ed) 1995 *Rhyme, Reading and Writing* Heinemann
Britton *et al*. 1973 *Understanding Children's Writing* Penguin
Brownjohn, S 1980 *Does it Have to Rhyme?* Hodder and Stoughton
Bullock 1975 *Language for Life* HMSO
Bunting, R (2000) *Teaching about Language in the Primary Years*, 2nd edn, London: David Fulton Publishers
Fisher, R and Williams, M (eds) (2000) *Unlocking Literacy, A Guide for Teachers,* London: David Fulton Publishers
Gilmour, M 1997 *Shakespeare for All in Primary Schools* Cassell
Goodwin, P (ed.) (1999) *The Literate Classroom*, London: David Fulton Publishers
Grugeon, E & Gardner, P (2000) *The Art of Storytelling for Teachers and Pupils*, London: David Fulton Publishers
Hackman, S & Trickett, L 1996 *Spelling 9-13* Hodder and Stoughton
Harrison, C & Coles, M (eds) 1992 *The Reading for Real Handbook* Routledge
Hornsby, B & Shear, F 1974 *Alpha to Omega: The A-Z of Teaching Reading, Writing and Spelling* Heinemann
Hughes, T 1967 *Poetry in the Making* Faber
Johnson, P (1993) *Literacy Through The Book Arts*, Hodder and Stoughton.
Lloyd, P, Michelle, H and Monk J (1999) *The Literacy Hour and Language Knowledge,* London: David Fulton Publishers
Marriott, S 1995 *Read On: Using Fiction in the Primary School* Chapman
Opie, I & Opie, P 1959 *The Lore and Language of Schoolchildren* OUP
Peer, L, and Reid, G (eds) (2000) *Multilingualism, Literacy and Dyslexia*, London: David Fulton Publishers
Ramsden, M 1993 *Rescuing Spelling* Southgate
Sassoon, R 1990 *Handwriting: the way to teach it* Leopard Learning
Styles, M & Triggs, P (eds) (1988) *Poetry 5-16* Books For Keeps
Vygotsky L 1978 *Mind in Society: The Development of Higher Psychological Processes* Harvard University Press
Wray, D & Medwell, J 1997 *English for Primary Teachers* Letts

Teaching resources for the classroom

Barker, R & Fidge, L 1998 *Key Stage 2: Literacy Activity Books (Year 3 – 6)* Letts
Barker, R & Franklin, G 1998 *Developing Literacy Skills: Spelling* (3 books, one each for Key Stage 1, Key Stage Y3–4 and Key Stage 2 Y 5–6) Hopscotch Educational Publishing
Barker, R & Fidge, L *1999 Differentiated Activity Books Word Level (Years 3–6)* Letts
Barker, R & Fidge, L *1999 Differentiated Activity Books Sentence Level (Years 3–6)* Letts
Barker, R & Fidge, L *1999 Focus on Writing Composition (Years 1–6)* Nelson

Barker, R & Moorcroft, C 1998 *Developing Literacy: Word Level, Years R – 6* A & C Black
Barker, R & Moorcroft, C 2000 *Developing Literacy: Text Level,* A & C Black
Fidge, L 1993 *Ideas Bank: Telling Stories, Key Stage 1* Folens
Fidge, L 1997 *Primary Grammar and Punctuation Books 1 – 4* Collins
Franklin, G & Barker, R 1998 *Bangers and Mash Teacher's Resource Book* Longman
Hopcroft, L 1998 *Developing Literacy Skills: Grammar, Key Stage 1* Hopscotch Educational Publishing
Hughes, P 1998 *Developing Literacy Skills: Using Stories, Key Stage 1 (P1–3)* Hopscotch
Johnson, P 1990 *A Book of One's Own* Hodder & Stoughton
Johnson, P 1992 *Pop-up Paper Engineering* Falmer
Mackay, F 1998 *Developing Literacy Skills: Using Stories* (2 books, one each for Key Stage Y3–4 and Key Stage 2 Y 5–6) Hopscotch Educational Publishing
Mackay, F 1998 *Developing Literacy Skills: Using Non-fiction* (2 books, one each for Key Stage 2 Y3–4 and Key Stage 2 Y 5–6) Hopscotch Educational Publishing
Mackay, F 1999 *Developing Literacy Skills: Using Poetry* (3 books, one each for Key Stage 1, Key Stage 2 Y3–4 and Key Stage 2 Y 5–6) Hopscotch Educational Publishing
Moorcroft, C 1999 *Key Stage 2 Revision Notes: English* Letts
Moorcroft, C 1999 *Developing Literacy: Sentence Level, Years R–6* A & C Black
Moorcroft, C 2000 *Developing Literacy: Poetry, Years R–6* A & C Black
Pattinson, M 1998 *Developing Literacy Skills: Grammar* (2 books, one each for Key Stage 2 Y3–4 and Key Stage 2 Y 5–6) Hopscotch Educational Publishing
Ray, R 1996 *Ideas Bank: Telling Stories, Key Stage 1* Folens
Redfern, A 1998 *Developing Literacy Skills: Using Non-fiction* Key Stage 1 Hopscotch Educational Publishing

Poetry anthologies

Ahlberg, A 1984 *Please Mrs Butler* Puffin
Beck, I 1997 *The Oxford Nursery Book* Oxford
Davies, N & Rae, S (eds) 1993 *Welcome to the Party* BBC
Eliot, T S 1986 *Old Possum's Book of Practical Cats* Faber & Faber
Harvey, A 1991 *Shades of Green* Red Fox
Heaney, S & Hughes, T (eds) 1997 *The School Bag* Faber & Faber
Hughes, S 1997 *The Nursery Collection* Walker
Hunt, R 1996 *Rockpool Rap* Oxford
McGough, R 1983 *Sky in the Pie* Penguin
Morgan, G (ed) 1998 *Read Me: A Poem a Day for the National Year of Reading*, Macmillan
Morgan, G (ed) 1999 *Read Me 2: A Poem a Day for the National Year of Reading*, Macmillan
Opie, I & Opie, P 1997 *The Oxford Nursery Rhyme Book* Oxford
Philip, N 1996 *The New Oxford Book of Children's Verse* Oxford

Appendix 2: Guidance on the objectives and study resources for each chapter

Chapter 1

Objectives
To gain an understanding of the changes which have taken place in the way English is taught in primary schools and of the factors which have influenced those changes.

Task 1 Reading

Graham, J & Kelly, A (2000) Reading Under Control, 2nd edn, London: David Fulton Publishers, chapter 1.

Graham, J & Kelly, A (1998) Writing Under Control, London: David Fulton Publishers, chapters 1 & 2.

Wray, D & Medwell, J (1998) Teaching English in Primary Schools, London: Letts, pp 6–10.

Task 2 Reading

Graham, J & Kelly, A (2000) Reading Under Control, 2nd edn, London: David Fulton Publishers, chapter 1.

Graham, J & Kelly, A (1998) Writing Under Control, London: David Fulton Publishers, chapters 1 & 2.

Audio-visual

DfEE (1998) *Literacy Training Pack Video 1*, Sequence 1 (The Introduction by The Secretary of State for Education, David Blunkett).

Task 3 Reading

DFE (1995) *The National Curriculum*, London: HMSO, pp v, 1–16.

DfEE (2000) *The National Curriculum*, London: HMSO, pp 11–13, pp 44-45.

Graham, J & Kelly, A (2000) Reading Under Control, 2nd edn, London: David Fulton Publishers, chapter 1.

Grugeon, E et al. (1998) Teaching Speaking and Listening in the Primary School, London: David Fulton Publishers, Introduction, chapter 1.

Books and other resources

DFE (1995) *The National Curriculum*, London: HMSO.

DfEE (2000) *The National Curriculum*, London: HMSO.

DfEE (1998) *Literacy Training Pack Video 1*, London: HMSO.

Graham, J & Kelly, A (2000) Reading Under Control, 2nd edn, London: David Fulton Publishers.

Graham, J & Kelly, A (1998) Writing Under Control, London: David Fulton Publishers.

Grugeon, E, Hubbard, L, Smith, C & Dawes, L(1998) Teaching Speaking and Listening in the Primary School, London: David Fulton Publishers.

Wray, D & Medwell, J (1998) Teaching English in Primary Schools, London: Letts.

Chapter 2

Objectives
To develop an appreciation of the value of stories in motivating children to read and in developing their reading and writing skills.

Task 1 Reading

Almond, David (1998) *Skellig,* Hodder (Whitbread Prize for Children's Fiction).
Waddell, Martin (1988) *Can't You Sleep, Little Bear?* Walker (Smarties Prize Grand Prix Winner and the Library Association Kate Greenaway Medal).

Task 2 Reading

Graham, J & Kelly, A (2000) Reading Under Control, 2nd edn, London: David Fulton Publishers, pp 19–20, 23–26, 72–76.

Task 3 Reading

DfEE (1998) *Literacy Training Pack, Module 4: Shared and Guided Reading and Writing at Pre-Key Stage 1* and *Module 5: Shared and Guided Reading and Writing at Key Stage 1 and Key Stage 2, Activity Resource Sheets,* London: HMSO.
Phinn, G (2000) Young Readers and their Books, London: David Fulton Publishers.

Books and other resources

Almond, David (1998) *Skellig,* Hodder.
DfEE (1998) *The National Literacy Strategy Framework for Teaching,* London: HMSO.
DfEE (1998) *Literacy Training Pack, Module 4: Shared and Guided Reading and Writing at Pre-Key Stage 1* and *Module 5 Shared and Guided Reading and Writing at Key Stage 1 and Key Stage 2, Activity Resource Sheets,* London: HMSO
Graham, J & Kelly, A (2000) Reading Under Control, 2nd edn, London: David Fulton Publishers.
Graham, J & Kelly, A (1998) Writing Under Control, London: David Fulton Publishers.
Waddell, Martin (1988) *Can't You Sleep, Little Bear?*, Walker.
Wray, D & Medwell J (1998) Teaching English in Primary Schools, London: Letts.

Chapter 3

Objectives
To gain an understanding of the reasons for, and purposes of, the National Literacy Strategy.
To become familiar with the structure and content of the National Literacy Strategy.

Task 1 Reading

DfEE (1998) *The National Literacy Strategy Framework for Teaching,* London: HMSO, pp 1–7.
Your notes from Chapter 1.

Task 2 Reading

DfEE (1998) *The National Literacy Strategy Framework for Teaching,* London: HMSO, pp 8–13.
DfEE (1998) *Literacy Training Pack, Module 1: The Literacy Hour, Teachers' Notes,* pp 4–5.
DfEE (1998) *Literacy Training Pack, Module 1: The Literacy Hour, Practical Suggestions for Organised Directed Independent Work,* pp 2–13.

Audio-visual

DfEE (1998) *Literacy Training Pack, Video 1, Module 1:* Sequences 2–3, 5.
DfEE (1998) *Literacy Training Pack, Module 1: The Literacy Hour, Cassette 1.*

Task 3 Reading

DfEE (1998) *The National Literacy Strategy Framework for Teaching*, pp 9–14.
DfEE (1998) *Literacy Training Pack, Module 1: The Literacy Hour, Teachers' Notes*, p 5.
Your notes on your observation of a Literacy Hour in a school.
Merchant, G & Thomas H (eds) (1999) *Picture Books for the Literacy Hour*, London: David Fulton
  Publishers.

Books and other resources

DfEE (1998) *The National Literacy Strategy Framework for Teaching*.
DfEE (1998) *Literacy Training Pack, Module 1: The Literacy Hour, Teachers' Notes*.
DfEE (1998) *Literacy Training Pack, Module 1: The Literacy Hour, Practical Suggestions for Organised
  Directed Independent Work*.
DfEE (1998) *Literacy Training Pack, Video 1*.
Wray, D & Medwell, J (1998) Teaching English in Primary Schools, London: Letts.

Chapter 4

Objectives

To become familiar with different methods of teaching reading, the reasons for them and
  their purposes. To gain knowledge of how to manage these methods in the classroom. To
  gain an understanding of the methods used in the Literacy Hour.

Task 1 Reading

DfEE (1998) *The National Literacy Strategy Framework for Teaching*, pp 8–13.
DfEE (1998) *Literacy Training Pack, Module 1: The Literacy Hour, Teachers' Notes* pp 4–5.
Wray, D & Medwell, J (1998) Teaching English in Primary Schools, London: Letts, pp 6–17.

Audio-visual

DfEE (1998) *Literacy Training Pack Video 1: Module 1*, Sequences 2–5.

Task 2 Reading

Branston, P & Provis, M (1999) *Children and Parents Enjoying Reading*, London: David Fulton
  Publishers.
**Graham, J & Kelly, A (2000) Reading Under Control, 2nd edn, London: David Fulton Publishers,
  pp 2–6, 11–14.**

Task 3 Reading

DfEE (1998) *The National Literacy Strategy Framework for Teaching*, pp 3–5.
Your Reading Journal.

Books and other resources

DfEE (1998) *The National Literacy Strategy Framework for Teaching*.
DfEE (1998) *The Literacy Training Pack, Video 1*.
Graham, J & Kelly, A (2000) Reading Under Control, 2nd edn, London: David Fulton Publishers.
Wray, D & Medwell J (1998) The Teaching of English in Primary Schools, London: Letts.

Chapter 5

Objectives
To gain an understanding of the ways in which teachers can use shared texts to teach important skills in reading and of what constitutes good practice in shared reading.

Task 1 Reading

DfEE (1998) *Literacy Training Pack, Module 4: Shared and Guided Reading at Pre-Key Stage 1 and Key Stage 1, Teachers' Notes*, pp 5–6, 8–9.

DfEE (1998) *Literacy Training Pack, Module 5: Shared and Guided Reading at Key Stage 2, Teachers' Notes*, pp 12–14.

Graham, J & Kelly, A (2000) Reading Under Control, 2nd edn, London: David Fulton Publishers, pp 68–71.

Wray, D & Medwell, J (1998) Teaching English in Primary Schools, London: Letts, pp 44–45, 49–51.

Audio-visual

DfEE (1998) *Literacy Training Pack, Video 2, Module 4*, Sequences 1–2 (Key Stage 1) .

DfEE (1998) *Literacy Training Pack, Video 2, Module 5*, Sequences 1, 4 (Key Stage 2).

Task 2 Reading

DfEE (1998) *The National Literacy Strategy Framework for Teaching*, pp 16–55.

DfEE (1998) *Literacy Training Pack, Module 4: Shared and Guided Reading at Pre-Key Stage 1 and Key Stage 1, Teachers' Notes*, pp 13–16, 38–41.

DfEE (1998) *Literacy Training Pack, Module 5: Shared and Guided Reading at Key Stage 2, Teachers' Notes*, pp 17–19, 26, 36–37.

Graham, J & Kelly, A (2000) Reading Under Control, 2nd edn, London: David Fulton Publishers, pp 27–28.

Wray, D & Medwell, J (1998) Teaching English in Primary Schools, London: Letts, pp 47–51.

Books and other resources

DfEE (1998) *The National Literacy Strategy Framework for Teaching*.

DfEE (1998) *Literacy Training Pack, Module 4: Shared and Guided Reading at Pre-Key Stage 1 and Key Stage 1, Teachers' Notes*.

DfEE (1998) *Literacy Training Pack, Module 5: Shared and Guided Reading at Key Stage 2 (Fiction and Poetry), Teachers' Notes*.

DfEE (1998) *Literacy Training Pack, Video 2*.

Graham, J & Kelly, A (2000) Reading Under Control, 2nd edn, London: David Fulton Publishers.

Grugeon, E and Gardner, P (2000) The Art of Storytelling for Teachers and Pupils, London: David Fulton Publishers.

Phinn, G, (2000) Young Readers and their Books, London: David Fulton Publishers.

Wray, D & Medwell, J (1998) Teaching English in Primary Schools, London: Letts.

Chapter 6

Objectives
To gain an understanding of the place of guided reading in teaching children to read and in extending their reading skills.

Task 1 Reading

DfEE (1998) *The National Literacy Strategy Framework for Teaching*, pp 18–19, 26–31 (Key Stage 1), pp 36–43, 50–55 (Key Stage 2), but mainly the autumn term's work.

Audio-visual

DfEE (1998) *Literacy Training Pack, Video 2, Module 4,* Sequence 1 (Key Stage 1).
DfEE (1998) *Literacy Training Pack, Video 2, Module 5,* Sequence 1 (Key Stage 2).

Task 2 Reading

DfEE (1998) *Literacy Training Pack, Module 4: Shared and Guided Reading at Pre-Key Stage 1 and Key Stage 1, Teachers' Notes,* pp 17, 42–44.
DfEE (1998) *Literacy Training Pack, Module 5: Shared and Guided Reading at Key Stage 2 (Fiction and Poetry), Teachers' Notes,* p 14 (OHT 5.4), pp 15–17 (Commentary).
Graham, J & Kelly, A (2000) Reading Under Control, 2nd edn, London: David Fulton Publishers, pp 94–101.
Wray, D & Medwell, J (1998) Teaching English in Primary Schools, London: Letts, pp 62–66.

Audio-visual

DfEE (1998) *Literacy Training Pack, Video 2, Module 4,* Sequences 1, 3 (Key Stage 1).
DfEE (1998) *Literacy Training Pack, Video 2, Module 5,* Sequences 2, 3 (Key Stage 2).

Task 3 Reading

DfEE (1998) *The National Literacy Strategy Framework for Teaching,* pp 16–55.
Carter, D (2000) Teaching Fiction in the Primary School, London: David Fulton Publishers.
Wray, D & Medwell, J (1998) Teaching English in Primary Schools, London: Letts, pp 59–62.

Books and other resources

DfEE (1998) *The National Literacy Strategy Framework for Teaching.*
DfEE (1998) *Literacy Training Pack, Module 4: Shared and Guided Reading at Pre-Key Stage 1 and Key Stage 1, Teachers' Notes.*
DfEE (1998) *Literacy Training Pack, Module 5: Shared and Guided Reading at Key Stage 2 (Fiction and Poetry), Teachers' Notes.*
DfEE (1998) *Literacy Training Pack, Video 2.*
Fountas, I.C. and Pinnell, G.S. (1996) *Guided Reading,* Heinemann.
Graham, J & Kelly, A (2000) Reading Under Control, 2nd edn, London: David Fulton Publishers.
Wray, D & Medwell, J (1998) Teaching English in Primary Schools, London: Letts.

Chapter 7

Objectives
To become familiar with the different genres of writing and their essential characteristics. To develop an awareness of the possible purposes, contexts and audiences for which children can write.

Task 1 Reading

Non-book texts, such as newspapers, advertisement posters, leaflets, brochures and photographs of signs and notices.

Task 2 Reading

DfEE (1998) *The National Literacy Strategy Framework for Teaching.*
Any play written for children: for example, *The Thwarting of Baron Bolligrew* (Robert Bolt), *It's too Frightening for Me!* (Shirley Hughes); or plays from reading schemes such as *Story Chest, All Aboard, Oxford Reading Tree, Playhouse* (Nelson); plays for infants (e.g. *Traditional Tales* (Ginn), *Sunshine Plays* (Heinemann), *Whodunnits* (Collins) or *Longman Book Project).*

Task 3 Reading

DfEE (1998) *The National Literacy Strategy Framework for Teaching*, pp 18–55, Writing composition (fiction and non-fiction).
DfEE (1998) *Literacy Training Pack, Modules 3–6, Activity Resource Sheets.*
Graham, J & Kelly, A (1998) Writing Under Control, London: David Fulton Publishers, chapter 4.
Wray, D & Medwell, J (1998) Teaching English in Primary Schools, London: Letts, pp 82–95.

Books and other resources

DfEE (1998) *The National Literacy Strategy Framework for Teaching.*
DfEE (1998) *Literacy Training Pack, Modules 3 – 6, Activity Resource Sheets.*
Graham, J & Kelly, A (1998) Writing Under Control, London: David Fulton Publishers.
Wray, D & Medwell, J (1998) Teaching English in Primary Schools, London: Letts.

> #### Chapter 8
>
> #### Objectives
> To gain an understanding of shared writing. To learn how to encourage full participation from the children in shared writing, and to help them to feel pride in what they have produced.

Task 1 Reading

DfEE (1998) *Literacy Training Pack, Module 4: Shared and Guided Reading and Writing at Pre-Key Stage 1 and Key Stage 1, Teachers' Notes*, pp 24–27, 44–52.
DfEE (1998) *Literacy Training Pack, Module 5: Shared and Guided Reading and Writing at Key Stage 2 (Fiction and Poetry), Teachers' Notes*, pp 20–23, 41–46.
Graham, J & Kelly, A (1998) Writing Under Control, London: David Fulton Publishers, chapter 2.
Wray, D & Medwell, J (1998) Teaching English in Primary Schools, London: Letts, pp 45–47.

Audio-visual

DfEE (1998) *Literacy Training Pack, Video 2, Module 4,* Sequence 4 (Key Stage 1).
DfEE (1998) *Literacy Training Pack, Video 2, Module 5,* Sequence 5 (Key Stage 2).

Task 2 Reading

DfEE (1998) *The National Literacy Strategy Framework for Teaching*, pp 16–55.
DfEE (1998) *Literacy Training Pack, Module 4: Shared and Guided Reading at Pre-Key Stage 1 and Key Stage 1, Teachers' Notes*, pp 26–30.
DfEE (1998) *Literacy Training Pack, Module 5: Shared and Guided Reading at Key Stage 2, Teachers' Notes*, pp 20–23.
Wray, D & Medwell, J (1997) English for Primary Teachers, London: Letts, pp 44–51.

Books and other resources

DfEE (1998) *The National Literacy Strategy Framework for Teaching.*
DfEE (1998) *Literacy Training Pack, Module 4: Shared and Guided Reading and Writing at Pre-Key Stage 1 and Key Stage 1, Teachers' Notes.*
DfEE (1998) *Literacy Training Pack, Module 5: Shared and Guided Reading and Writing at Key Stage 2 (Fiction and Poetry), Teachers' Notes.*
DfEE (1998) *Literacy Training Pack, Video 2.*
Evans, J (ed.) (2000) *The Writing Classroom*, London: David Fulton Publishers.
Graham, J & Kelly, A (1998) Writing Under Control, London: David Fulton Publishers.
Wray, D & Medwell, J (1998) Teaching English in Primary Schools, London: Letts.

Chapter 9

Objectives
To gain an understanding of the value of guided writing in teaching children to write and in extending their writing skills.

Task 1 Reading

DfEE (1998) *Literacy Training Pack, Module 4: Shared and Guided Reading and Writing at Pre-Key Stage 1 and Key Stage 1, Teachers' Notes*, pp 26–27, 44–51 and *Activity Resource Sheets.*
DfEE (1998) *Literacy Training Pack, Module 5: Shared and Guided Reading and Writing at Key Stage 2 (Fiction and Poetry), Teachers' Notes*, pp 23–24, 27, 42–47 and *Activity Resource Sheets.*
Graham, J & Kelly, A (1998) Writing Under Control, London: David Fulton Publishers, chapter 2.
Wray, D & Medwell, J (1998) Teaching English in Primary Schools, London: Letts, pp 62–63.

Audio-visual

DfEE (1998) *Literacy Training Pack, Video 2, Module 4, Sequence 5 (Key Stage 1), Module 5, Sequence 6 (Key Stage 2).*

Task 2 Reading

DfEE (1998) *The National Literacy Strategy Framework for Teaching*, pp 16–55.
DfEE (1998) *Literacy Training Pack, Module 4: Shared and Guided Reading and Writing at Pre-Key Stage 1 and Key Stage 1, Teachers' Notes*, pp 44–51.
DfEE (1998) *Literacy Training Pack, Module 5: Shared and Guided Reading and Writing at Key Stage 2 (Fiction and Poetry), Teachers' Notes*, p 27.
Wray, D & Medwell, J (1998) Teaching English in Primary Schools, London: Letts, pp 66–69.

Books and other resources

DfEE (1998) *The National Literacy Strategy Framework for Teaching.*
DfEE (1998) *Literacy Training Pack, Module 4: Shared and Guided Reading and Writing at Pre-Key Stage 1 and Key Stage 1, Teachers' Notes, and Activity Resource Sheets.*
DfEE (1998) *Literacy Training Pack, Module 5: Shared and Guided Reading and Writing at Key Stage 2 (Fiction and Poetry), Teachers' Notes, and Activity Resource Sheets.*
DfEE (1998) *Literacy Training Pack, Video 2.*
Graham, J & Kelly, A (1998) Writing Under Control, London: David Fulton Publishers.
Wray, D & Medwell, J (1998) Teaching English in Primary Schools, London: Letts.

Chapter 10

Objectives
To gain an understanding of the word-level strategies used in reading and of the terminology used to describe them.

Task 1 Reading

DfEE (1998) *Literacy Training Pack, Module 2: Word-Level Work, Unit 1, Teachers' Notes*, pp 7–13.

Audio-visual

DfEE (1998) *Literacy Training Pack*, Audio Cassette 1 (Side 1): Word-Level Work.

Books and other resources

DfEE (1998) *The National Literacy Strategy Framework for Teaching.*
DfEE (1998) *Literacy Training Pack, Module 2: Word-Level Work, Units 1–2, Teachers' Notes and Activity Resource Sheets.*

DfEE (1998) *Literacy Training Pack, Audio Cassettes 1, 2.*
DfEE (1998) *Literacy Training Pack, Video 1.*
Graham, J & Kelly, A (2000) Reading Under Control, 2nd edn, London: David Fulton Publishers.
Layton, L, Deeny, K and Upton, G (1997) *Sound Practice - Phonological Awareness in the Classroom,* London: David Fulton Publishers.
Pinnell, G.S. and Fountas, I. (1998) *Words Matter,* Heinemann.
Wray, D & Medwell, J (1998) Teaching English in Primary Schools, London: Letts.

Task 2 Reading

DfEE (1998) *Literacy Training Pack, Module 2: Word-Level Work, Unit 2, Teachers' Notes,* pp 8–12 (Activities 1 and 2), 13, 16–17, 19–24 (omitting the activities on assessment, which is covered in Chapter 12).
DfEE (1998) *Literacy Training Pack, Module 2: Word-Level Work, Activity Resource Sheets.*
Graham, J & Kelly, A (2000) Reading Under Control, 2nd edn, London: David Fulton Publishers, pp 82–93.
Wray, D & Medwell, J (1998) Teaching English in Primary Schools, London: Letts, pp 52, 54–57.

Audio-visual

DfEE (1998) *Literacy Training Pack, Video 1, Module 2, Sequences 1 – 5.*

Task 3 Reading

DfEE (1998) *The National Literacy Strategy Framework for Teaching,* pp 18–55 (word-level: word-recognition and vocabulary extension), 60–63.
DfEE (1998) *Literacy Training Pack, Module 2: Word-Level Work, Unit 2, Activity Resource Sheets,* pp 6–7, 13–15, 17–19, 24, 80, 84–88, 94, 105.
Graham, J & Kelly, A (2000) Reading Under Control, 2nd edn, London: David Fulton Publishers, pp 144–146.
Wray, D & Medwell, J (1998) Teaching English in Primary Schools, London: Letts, pp 107–111, 114–115.

Audio-visual

DfEE (1998) *Literacy Training Pack, Video 1, Module 2, Sequences 6–7.*

Chapter 11

Objectives
To gain an understanding of the sentence-level strategies which are used in reading and writing.
To become aware of effective methods for teaching children about grammar, sentence-structure and punctuation, including marking their work.

Task 1 Reading

DfEE (1998) *The National Literacy Strategy Framework for Teaching,* pp 18–55.
DfEE (1998) *Literacy Training Pack, Module 2: Word-Level Work, Unit 1, Teachers' Notes,* pp 7–13.

Audio-visual

DfEE (1998) *Literacy Training Pack, Audio Cassette 1, Module 2, Side 1.*

Task 2 Reading

DfEE (1998) *Literacy Training Pack, Module 3: Sentence-Level Work, Teachers' Notes,* pp 17–22, 27–30, 33–35.
Pollock, J and Waller, E (1999) English Grammar and Teaching Strategies, London: David Fulton Publishers.
Wilson, A (1999) Language Knowledge for Primary Teachers, London: David Fulton Publishers.

Audio-visual

DfEE (1998) *Literacy Training Pack Video 2, Module 3: Sequences 3, 5.*

Task 3 Reading

DfEE (1998) *Literacy Training Pack, Module 3: Sentence-Level Work, Teachers' Notes*, pp 35–39.
Graham, J & Kelly, A (1998) *Writing Under Control*, London: David Fulton Publishers, pp 8, 11, 119.

Audio-visual

DfEE (1998) *Literacy Training Pack Video 2, Module 3: Sequence 6.*

Books and other resources

DfEE (1998) *The National Literacy Strategy Framework for Teaching.*
DfEE (1998) *Literacy Training Pack, Module 2: Word-Level Work, Unit 1, Teachers' Notes.*
DfEE (1998) *Literacy Training Pack, Module 3: Sentence-Level Work, Teachers' Notes.*
DfEE (1998) *Literacy Training Pack, Video 2.*
DfEE (1998) *Literacy Training Pack, Audio Cassette 1.*
Graham, J & Kelly, A (1998) *Writing Under Control*, London: David Fulton Publishers.

> **Chapter 12**
>
> **Objectives**
> To be familiar with the main types of assessment and their purposes and with methods of monitoring and recording children's progress.
> To be able to carry out miscue analysis.

Task 1 Reading

Graham, J & Kelly, A (2000) Reading Under Control, 2nd edn, London: David Fulton Publishers, pp 113–116, 127–134.
Wray, D & Medwell, J (1998) Teaching English in Primary Schools, London: Letts, pp 127–132.

Task 2 Reading

Graham, J & Kelly, A (2000) Reading Under Control, 2nd edn, London: David Fulton Publishers, pp 114–116.
Wray, D & Medwell, J (1998) Teaching English in Primary Schools, London: Letts, pp 62–66.

Task 3 Reading

DfEE (1998) *Literacy Training Pack, Module 2: Word Level Work, Unit 2, Teachers' Notes*, pp 17–19, 47–61.
Carter, D (2000) Teaching Fiction in The Primary School, London: David Fulton Publishers, Part 6.

Audio-visual

DfEE (1998) *Literacy Training Pack, Video 1: Sequence 3.*

Task 4 Reading

Graham, J & Kelly, A (2000) Reading Under Control, 2nd edn, London: David Fulton Publishers, pp 116–127.
Wray, D & Medwell, J (1998) Teaching English in Primary Schools, London: Letts, pp 133–137, 169.

Books and other resources

DfEE (1998) *The National Literacy Strategy Framework for Teaching.*
DfEE (1998) *Literacy Training Pack, Module 2: Word Level Work, Unit 2, Teachers' Notes.*
DfEE (1998) *Literacy Training Pack, Video 1.*

Goodman, Y, Watson, D and Burke, C (1987) *Reading Miscue Inventory*. Owen.
Graham, J & Kelly, A (2000) Reading Under Control, 2nd edn, London: David Fulton Publishers.
Wray, D & Medwell, J (1998) Teaching English in Primary Schools, London: Letts.

Chapter 13

Objectives
To develop an ability to use appropriate methods for assessing children's attainment in writing.
To be able to assess children's writing against criteria and to use the assessment to inform teaching.

Task 1 Reading

DfEE (1998) *Literacy Training Pack, Module 3: Sentence Level Work, Teachers' Notes*, pp 13–16.

Task 2 Reading

Graham, J & Kelly, A (1998) Writing Under Control, London: David Fulton Publishers, pp 112–118, 119–124.

Task 3 Reading

DfE (1995) *The National Curriculum*, HMSO, pp1–16, 25–31 (English).
Wray, D & Medwell, J (1998) Teaching English in Primary Schools, London: Letts, pp 130–132.

Books and other resources

DfE (1995) *The National Curriculum*, HMSO.
DfEE (1998) *The National Literacy Strategy Framework for Teaching.*
DfEE (1998) *Literacy Training Pack, Module 3: Sentence Level Work, Teachers' Notes.*
Graham, J & Kelly, A (1998) Writing Under Control, London: David Fulton Publishers.
Wray, D & Medwell, J (1998) Teaching English in Primary Schools, London: Letts.

Chapter 14

Objectives
To develop skills in selecting texts from the appropriate range for an age group and identifying the text-, sentence- and word-level work which can be developed from them.
To develop skills in systematic planning to teach a class of children all the strands of the National Literacy Strategy specified for a term and to organise this planning into a weekly timetable.

Task 1 Reading

DfEE (1998) *The National Literacy Strategy Framework for Teaching*, pp 18–55, 58–59.
DfEE (1998) *Literacy Training Pack, Module 1: The Literacy Hour, Teachers' notes*, pp 26–29.

Task 2 Reading

DfEE (1998) *The National Literacy Strategy Framework for Teaching*, pp 18–55, 58–59.
DfEE (1998) *Literacy Training Pack, Module 4: Shared and Guided Reading and Writing at Pre-Key Stage 1 and Key Stage 1, Teachers' Notes*, pp 13–16, 20–22, 28–35 and *Activity Resource Sheets.*
DfEE (1998) *Literacy Training Pack, Module 5: Shared and Guided Reading and Writing at Key Stage 2, Teacher's Notes*, pp 38–40, and *Activity Resource Sheets.*

Books and other resources

DfEE (1998) *The National Literacy Strategy Framework for Teaching.*
DfEE (1998) *Literacy Training Pack, Module 1: The Literacy Hour.*
DfEE (1998) *Literacy Training Pack, Module 4: Shared and Guided Reading and Writing at Pre-Key Stage 1 and Key Stage 1, Teachers' Notes and Activity Resource Sheets.*

DfEE (1998) *Literacy Training Pack, Module 5: Shared and Guided Reading and Writing at Key Stage 2, Teacher's Notes and Activity Resource Sheets*.

Chapter 15

Objectives
To explore the presentation of texts of different genres, including information technology.
To be able to develop children's presentation skills, including handwriting, and their ability to consider the effect of the appearance of their writing on their audience.
To help children to select appropriate ways in which to present their work and to develop their skills in presentation.

Task 1 Reading

Graham, J & Kelly, A (1998) Writing Under Control, London: David Fulton Publishers, pp 103–110.
Godwin, D & Perkins, M (1998) Teaching Language and Literacy in the Early Years, London: David Fulton Publishers, chapter 6.

Task 2 Reading

DfEE (1998) *The National Literacy Strategy Framework for Teaching*, pp 18–55.
Doonan, J (1993) *Looking at Pictures in Picture Books*. London: Thimble Press.
Evans, J (1998) *What's in the Picture*, London: Paul Chapman.
Godwin, D & Perkins, M (1998) Teaching Language and Literacy in the Early Years, London: David Fulton Publishers, Figures 3.4, 6.1, 6.4, 6.6, 6.7, 6.11.
Graham, J (1990) *Pictures on the Page*, Sheffield: NATE.
Graham, J & Kelly, A (1998) Writing Under Control, London: David Fulton Publishers, pp 48–50.
Michaels, W and Walsh, M (1996) *Up and Away*, Oxford.

Task 3 Reading

DfEE (1998) *The National Literacy Strategy Framework for Teaching*, pp 5, 18–55.
Graham, J & Kelly, A (1998) Writing Under Control, London: David Fulton Publishers, pp 63–69.

Books and other resources

DfEE (1998) *The National Literacy Strategy Framework for Teaching*.
Godwin, D & Perkins, M (1998) Teaching Language and Literacy in the Early Years, London: David Fulton Publishers.
Graham, J & Kelly, A (1998) Writing Under Control, London: David Fulton Publishers.

Chapter 16

Objectives
To gain an awareness of the processes which can be used in the spelling of unknown words.
To be able to plan activities for teaching the spellings of irregular words and to help children to discover rules (and their exceptions) for spelling and to devise their own rules.

Task 1 Reading

DfEE (1998) *Literacy Training Pack Module 2, Teachers' Notes*, p 3.

Audio-visual

DfEE (1998) *Literacy Training Pack Audio Cassette 1*, Side 1

Books and other resources

DfEE (1998) *The National Literacy Strategy Framework for Teaching*.
DfEE (1998) *Literacy Training Pack Module 2: Word-Level Work, Unit 3: Spelling* and *Activity Resource Sheets*.

DfEE (1998) *Literacy Training Pack Audio Cassette 1.*
Graham, J & Kelly, A (1998) Writing Under Control, London: David Fulton Publishers.
Wray, D & Medwell, J (1998) Teaching English in Primary Schools, London: Letts.

Task 2 Reading

DfEE (1998) *The National Literacy Strategy Framework for Teaching,* pp 73–89.
DfEE (1998) *Literacy Training Pack, Module 2: Word-Level Work, Unit 3, Spelling,* pp 7–9 and *Activity Resource Sheets,* pp 6–7, 24, 82, 84–88, 94, 96, 97, 102–104, 109, 112, 124–127.
Graham, J & Kelly, A (1998) Writing Under Control, London: David Fulton Publishers, pp 23–25, 70–91.
Wray, D & Medwe!l, J (1998) Teaching English in Primary Schools, London: Letts, pp 51–57.

Task 3 Reading

DfEE (1998) *The National Literacy Strategy Framework for Teaching,* pp 18–55.
DfEE (1998) *Literacy Training Pack Module 2: Word-Level Work, Unit 3, Spelling, Teachers' Notes,* pp 8–26 and *Activity Resource Sheets,* pp 79–145.
Graham, J & Kelly, A (1998) Writing Under Control, London: David Fulton Publishers, chapter 5.
Wray, D & Medwell J (1998) Teaching English in Primary Schools, London: Letts, pp 51–57.

> **Chapter 17**
>
> **Objectives**
> To develop an understanding of the skills used in reading non-fiction texts.
> To be able to plan activities for the Literacy Hour in which the focus is the reading of non-fiction texts.

Task 1 Reading

DfEE (1998) *The National Literacy Strategy Framework for Teaching,* pp 18–55.
DfEE (1998) *Literacy Training Pack, Module 6: Reading and Writing for Information, Teacher's Notes,* pp 3–4.
Wray, D & Lewis, M (1997) Extending Literacy, London: Routledge, chapters 1–3.

Audio-visual

DfEE (1998) *Literacy Training Pack, Module 6, Audio Cassette 4,* Side 2.

Task 2 Reading

DfEE (1998) *The National Literacy Strategy Framework for Teaching,* pp 16–55.
DfEE (1998) *Literacy Training Pack, Module 6: Reading and Writing for Information, Teachers' Notes,* pp 8–15 and *Activity Resource Sheets,* pp 3–5, 7, 9, 11.
Graham, J & Kelly, A (2000) *Reading Under Control,* 2nd edn, London: David Fulton Publishers, pp 22–23, 98–99.
Wray, D & Lewis, M (1997) Extending Literacy, London: Routledge, chapters 5–8.
Wray, D & Medwell, J (1998) Teaching English in Primary Schools, London: Letts, pp 25–31, 69–74, 79–82, 165–166.

Audio-visual

DfEE (1998) *Literacy Training Pack, Module 6, Video 2, Sequences 2–3.*

Books and other resources

DfEE (1998) *The National Literacy Strategy Framework for Teaching.*
DfEE (1998) *Literacy Training Pack, Module 6: Reading and Writing for Information, Teacher's Notes* and *Activity Resource Sheets.*

DfEE (1998) *Literacy Training Pack, Video 2.*
DfEE (1998) *Literacy Training Pack, Audio Cassette 4.*
Graham, J & Kelly, A (2000) Reading Under Control, 2nd edn, London: David Fulton Publishers.
Wray, D, & Lewis, M (1997) Extending Literacy, London: Routledge.
Wray, D & Medwell, J (1998) Teaching English in Primary Schools, London: Letts.

Chapter 18

Objectives
To recognise the importance of non-fiction writing for children.
To develop an appreciation of the problems faced by children writing non-fiction and to be able to provide them with the support they need to overcome these problems.

Task 1 Reading

DfEE (1998) *The National Literacy Strategy Framework for Teaching*, pp 18–55.
DfEE (1998) *Literacy Training Pack, Module 6, Teachers' Notes*, p 16.

Task 2 Reading

DfEE (1998) *The National Literacy Strategy Framework for Teaching*, pp 18–55.
DfEE (1998) *Literacy Training Pack, Video 2, Module 6: Reading and Writing for Information,* Sequence 3.
Wray, D & Medwell, J (1998) Teaching English in Primary Schools, London: Letts, pp 25–35, 165.

Task 3 Reading

DfEE (1998) *Literacy Training Pack, Module 6: Reading and Writing for Information, Teachers' Notes*, pp 18–25, *Trainer's Notes*, pp 20–1, *Overhead Transparencies* 6.15–6.19 and *Activity Resource Sheets*, pp 8–23.
DfEE (1988) *Literacy Training Pack, Video 2, Module 6: Reading and Writing for Information,* Sequence 4.
Lewis, M & Wray, D (1996) *Writing Frames: scaffolding children's non-fiction writing in a range of genres*, University of Reading: Reading and Language Information Centre, pp 2–15.
Wray, D & Medwell, J (1998) Teaching English in Primary Schools, London: Letts, pp 25–35, 69–74, 79–82, 145–164.

Books and other resources

DfEE (1998) *The National Literacy Strategy Framework for Teaching.*
DfEE (1998) *Literacy Training Pack, Module 6, Teachers' Notes and Activity Resource Sheets.*
DfEE (1998) *Literacy Training Pack, Video 2.*
Lewis, M & Wray, D (1996), *Writing Frames: scaffolding children's non-fiction writing in a range of genres*, University of Reading: Reading and Language Information Centre.
Lewis, M & Wray, D (1995) *Developing children's non-fiction writing*, Leamington Spa: Scholastic.
Wray, D & Medwell, J (1998) Teaching English in Primary Schools, London: Letts.

Chapter 19

Objectives
To gain an understanding of the processes involved in taking notes and to be able to show children how to make organised and effective notes.
To be able to plan ways of teaching children to evaluate what they read (to recognise fact, opinion and bias).
To be able to model the processes of reviewing, revisiting and restructuring information in order to remember it.

Task 1 Reading

Brown, R (1994) *Ideas Bank: Information and Library Skills*, Dunstable: Folens, pp 34–4.
DfEE (2000) *The National Curriculum*, London: HMSO, pp 38, 46–49, pp 53–58.
DfEE (1998) *The National Literacy Strategy Framework for Teaching*, pp 18–55.
DfEE (1998) *Literacy Training Pack, Module 6: Reading and Writing for Information, Activity Resource Sheets*, p 13.
Wray, D & Lewis, M (1997) Extending Literacy, London: Routledge, chapter 8.
Wray, D & Medwell, J (1998) Teaching English in Primary Schools, London: Letts, pp 26, 80–81.

Task 2 Reading

Wray, D & Lewis, M (1997) Extending Literacy, London: Routledge, chapter 9.

Task 3 Reading

Wray, D & Lewis, M (1997) Extending Literacy, London: Routledge, pp 38, 82–91.
Moorcroft, C (1997a) Foundations for Reading: Essential Activities (Early), Dunstable: Folens, pp 14, 15, 18, 20–25, 29, 32, 33, 35, 38, 40–42, 44, 48, 51–53, 59, 60, 63, 67, 69, 70, 72, 73, 76, 78, 80–83, 85–87, 89, 91, 92.
Moorcroft, C (1997b) Foundations for Reading: Essential Activities (Experienced), Dunstable: Folens, pp 12, 13, 15, 16, 18, 19, 22–24, 26, 28–34, 38–43, 45.

Books and other resources

DfEE (2000) *The National Curriculum*, London: HMSO, pp 38, 46-49, 53-58.
DfEE (1998) *The National Literacy Strategy Framework for Teaching*.
DfEE (1998) *Literacy Training Pack, Module 6: Reading and Writing for Information, Activity Resource Sheets*.
Moorcroft, C (1997a) Foundations for Reading: Essential Activities (Early), Dunstable: Folens.
Moorcroft, C (1997b) Foundations for Reading: Essential Activities (Experienced), Dunstable: Folens.
Wray, D & Lewis, M (1997) Extending Literacy, London: Routledge.
Wray, D & Medwell, J (1998) Teaching English in Primary Schools, London: Letts.

Chapter 20

Objectives
To develop an awareness of the opportunities for speaking and listening which can be provided in English, and in other subjects, and of the role of the teacher and other adults in these discussions.
To be able to plan for children to take part in purposeful discussions and to develop their skills in story-telling.

Task 1 Reading

DfEE (2000) *The National Curriculum*, London: HMSO, pp 44–45, 50–52.
DfEE (1998) *The National Literacy Strategy Framework for Teaching*, pp 18–55.
Godwin, D & Perkins, M (1998) Teaching Language and Literacy in the Early Years, London: David Fulton Publishers, chapter 1.
Wray, D & Medwell, J (1998) Teaching English in Primary Schools, London: Letts, pp 35–40.

Task 2 Reading

Godwin, D & Perkins, M (1998) Teaching Language and Literacy in the Early Years, London: David Fulton Publishers, chapter 1.
Grugeon, E et al. (1998) Teaching Speaking and Listening in the Primary School, London: David Fulton Publishers, chapters 1–2, 4–5.
SCAA (1996) *Desirable Outcomes for Children's Learning on Entering Compulsory Education*, pp 3, 9–13.

Task 3 Reading

QCA/DfEE (2000) *Curriculum Guidance for the Foundation Stage*, London: QCA.
QCA (1999) *Teaching Speaking and Listening in Key Stages 1&2,* London: QCA.

Books and other resources

DfEE (2000) *The National Curriculum,* London: HMSO.
DfEE (1998) *The National Literacy Strategy Framework for Teaching.*
Godwin, D & Perkins, M (1998) Teaching Language and Literacy in the Early Years, London: David Fulton Publishers.
Grugeon, E & Gardner, P (2000) *The Art of Storytelling for Teachers and Pupils,* London: David Fulton Publishers.
Grugeon, E, Hubbard, L, Smith, C & Dawes, L (1998) Teaching Speaking and Listening in the Primary School, London: David Fulton Publishers.
SCAA (1996) *Desirable Outcomes for Children's Learning on Entering Compulsory Education,* London: DfEE.
Wray, D & Medwell, J (1998) Teaching English in Primary Schools, London: Letts.

Chapter 21

Objectives
To gain an appreciation of different forms of poetry and how these can be used in the primary classroom.
To consider the various devices used by poets.
To investigate some approaches to the reading and writing of poetry.

Task 1 Reading

Orme D & Andrew, M (1990) *The Poetry Kit*, Cheltenham: Stanley Thornes Publishers, Introduction.
Orme, D (1992) *The Essential Guide to Poetry*, Dunstable: Folens.
Carter, D (1998) Teaching Poetry in the Primary School, London: David Fulton Publishers, chapter 1.

Task 2 Reading

Carter, D (1998) Teaching Poetry in the Primary School, London: David Fulton Publishers, chapter 4, pp 133–143.
DfEE (1998) *Literacy Training Pack, Module 4: Shared and Guided Writing at Pre-Key Stage 1 and Key Stage 1, Teachers' Notes,* p 35, *Activity Resource Sheets,* pp 4, 6.
DfEE (1998) *Literacy Training Pack, Module 5: Shared and Guided Writing at Key Stage 2, Teacher's Notes,* pp 9–11, 29–32, Appendix 3, *Activity Resource Sheets,* pp 6, 13.
Grugeon, E et al. (1998) Teaching Speaking and Listening in the Primary School, London: David Fulton Publishers, pp 8–10, 40–48.

Task 3 Reading

DfEE (1998) *National Literacy Strategy Framework for Teaching,* pp 18–55 (Text-level strand: poetry objectives), 73–91.
DfEE (1998) *Literacy Training Pack, Module 4: Shared and Guided Writing at Pre-Key Stage 1 and Key Stage 1, Teachers' Notes,* p 35, *Activity Resource Sheets,* pp 4, 6.
DfEE (1998) *Literacy Training Pack, Module 5: Shared and Guided Writing at Key Stage 2, Teacher's Notes,* pp 9–11, 29–32, Appendix 3, *Activity Resource Sheets,* pp 6, 13.
Graham, J & Kelly, A (1998) Writing Under Control, London: David Fulton Publishers, pp 55–59.

Books and other resources

Carter, D (1998) Teaching Poetry in the Primary School, London: David Fulton Publishers.
DfEE (1998) *Literacy Training Pack, Module 4: Shared and Guided Writing at Pre-Key Stage 1 and Key Stage 1, Teachers' Notes* and *Activity Resource Sheets*.
DfEE (1998) *Literacy Training Pack, Module 5: Shared and Guided Writing at Key Stage 2, Teacher's Notes* and *Activity Resource Sheets*.
Grugeon, E *et al.* (1998) *Teaching Speaking and Listening in the Primary School*, London: David Fulton Publishers.
Orme, D & Andrew, M (1990) *The Poetry Kit*, Cheltenham: Stanley Thornes Publishers.
Orme, D (1992) *The Essential Guide to Poetry*, Dunstable: Folens.

Chapter 22

Objectives
To develop an awareness of the opportunities for drama which can be provided in English and in other subjects and to be able to plan learning activities which use drama to develop children's oracy and literacy.
To be able to plan learning activities which teach drama as a creative art in its own right.

Task 1 Reading

Clipson-Boyles, S (1998) Drama in Primary English Teaching, London: David Fulton Publishers, pp 6–7.
DFE (1995) *The National Curriculum,* London: HMSO, pp 1–16, 26–30.
DfEE (1998) *The National Literacy Strategy Framework for Teaching*, pp 18–55.

Task 2 Reading

Clipson-Boyles, S (1998) Drama in Primary English Teaching, London: David Fulton Publishers, chapter 3.
DfEE (1998) *The National Literacy Strategy Framework for Teaching*, pp 18–55.
Godwin, D & Perkins, M (1998) Teaching Language and Literacy in the Early Years, London: David Fulton Publishers, pp 48–50, 124–125.
Grugeon et al. (1998) Teaching Speaking and Listening in the Primary School, London: David Fulton Publishers, pp 121–124.
Graham, J & Kelly, A (2000) Reading Under Control, 2nd edn, London: David Fulton Publishers, pp 79–82.

Task 3 Reading

Clipson-Boyles, S (1998) Drama in Primary English Teaching, London: David Fulton Publishers, pp 22–25.

Books and other resources

Clipson-Boyles, S (1998) Drama in Primary English Teaching, London: David Fulton Publishers.
DFE (1995) *The National Curriculum,* London: HMSO.
DfEE (1998) *The National Literacy Strategy Framework for Teaching*.
Godwin, D & Perkins, M (1998) Teaching Language and Literacy in the Early Years, London: David Fulton Publishers.
Grugeon, E et al. (1998) Teaching Speaking and Listening in the Primary School, London: David Fulton Publishers.
Graham, J & Kelly, A (2000) Reading Under Control, 2nd edn, London: David Fulton Publishers.
Winston, J (2000) *Drama, Literacy and Moral Education 5-11*, London: David Fulton Publishers.

Chapter 23

Objectives
To gain an appreciation of the contribution which parents and other members of children's families can make to their progress in English.
To be able to plan and organise the assistance of other adults in the teaching of English.

Task 1 Reading

Graham, J & Kelly, A (2000) Reading Under Control, 2nd edn, London: David Fulton Publishers, p 109.
Godwin, D & Perkins, M (1998) Teaching Language and Literacy in the Early Years, London: David Fulton Publishers, pp 105–107, 110–114.

Task 2 Reading

Godwin, D & Perkins, M (1998) Teaching Language and Literacy in the Early Years, London: David Fulton Publishers, pp 116–119.
Graham, J & Kelly, A (2000) Reading Under Control, 2nd edn, London: David Fulton Publishers, pp 109–112.
Graham, J & Kelly, A (1998) Writing Under Control, London: David Fulton Publishers, pp 38–39.
SCAA (1996) *Desirable Outcomes for Children's Learning on Entering Compulsory Education*, London: DfEE, p 7.
Wolfendale, S and Bastiani, J (2000) *The Contribution of Parents to School Effectiveness*, London: David Fulton Publishers.

Task 3 Reading

Clipson-Boyles, S (1996) *Supporting Language and Literacy*, London: David Fulton Publishers.
Godwin, D & Perkins, M (1998) Teaching Language and Literacy in the Early Years, London: David Fulton Publishers, pp 107–110.

Books and other resources

Branston, P & Provis, M (1999) *Children and Parents Enjoying Reading,* London: David Fulton Publishers.
DfEE (1998) *The National Literacy Strategy Framework for Teaching.*
Godwin, D & Perkins, M (1998) Teaching Language and Literacy in the Early Years, London: David Fulton Publishers.
Graham, J & Kelly, A (2000) Reading Under Control, 2nd edn, London: David Fulton Publishers.
Grugeon, E et al. (1998) Teaching Speaking and Listening in the Primary School, London: David Fulton Publishers.
SCAA (1996) *Desirable Outcomes for Children's Learning on Entering Compulsory Education*, London: DfEE.

Chapter 24

Objectives
To gain an appreciation of the needs of children whose home and community language is not English.
To be able to plan appropriate learning experiences for these children.

Task 1 Reading

Bastiani, J (ed.) *Home-School Work in Multi-Cultural Settings*, London: David Fulton Publishers.
Clipson-Boyles, S (1998) Drama in Primary English Teaching, London: David Fulton Publishers, pp 77–79.

Graham, J & Kelly, A (1998) Writing Under Control, London: David Fulton Publishers, pp 134–135.

SCAA (1996) *Teaching English as an Additional Language*, London: DfEE, p 7.

QCA / DfEE (2000) *Curriculum Guidance for the Foundation Stage*, London: QCA.

Task 2 Reading

Clipson-Boyles, S (1998) Drama in Primary English Teaching, London: David Fulton Publishers, chapter 9.

Graham, J & Kelly, A (2000) Reading Under Control, 2nd edn, London: David Fulton Publishers, pp 7–8.

Graham, J & Kelly, A (1998) Writing Under Control, London: David Fulton Publishers, pp 10–11, 47, 74–77, 133–139.

Grugeon, E et al. (1998) Teaching Speaking and Listening in the Primary School, London: David Fulton Publishers, pp 15–16, 30–31, 43.

OFSTED (1994) *Spiritual, Moral, Social and Cultural Education*, London: OFSTED, pp 8–10, 15–18.

Task 3 Reading

Clipson-Boyles, S (1998) Drama in Primary English Teaching, London: David Fulton Publishers, pp 80–83.

Graham, J & Kelly, A (2000) Reading Under Control, 2nd edn, London: David Fulton Publishers, pp 39–43.

Grugeon, E *et al.* (1998) *Teaching Speaking and Listening in the Primary School*, London: David Fulton Publishers, pp 29–31.

Dual-language books and texts in other languages commonly spoken in schools in Britain.

Books and other resources

Clipson-Boyles, S (1998) Drama in Primary English Teaching, London: David Fulton Publishers.

DfEE (2000) *The National Curriculum,* London: HMSO.

Gibbons, P (1996) *Learning to Learn in a Second Language*, PETA.

Graham, J & Kelly, A (2000) Reading Under Control, 2nd edn, London: David Fulton Publishers.

Graham, J & Kelly, A (1998) Writing Under Control, London: David Fulton Publishers.

Grugeon, E et al. (1998) Teaching Speaking and Listening in the Primary School, London: David Fulton Publishers.

OFSTED (1994) *Spiritual, Moral, Social and Cultural Education*, London: OFSTED.

SCAA (1996) *Teaching English as an Additional Language*, London: DfEE.

Chapter 25

Objectives

To gain an understanding of the types of assessment which are likely to be helpful in identifying special educational needs in English

To be able to plan learning experiences (with the support of specialists where appropriate) which will help children with special educational needs to make the best possible progress in English.

Task 1 Reading

DFE Circular 6/94, *Code of Practice on the Identification and Assessment of Special Educational Needs*, London: HMSO.

Graham, J & Kelly, A (2000) Reading Under Control, 2nd edn, London: David Fulton Publishers, pp 113, 127–130, 141–142.

Worthington, A (1999) *The Fulton Special Education Digest,* London: David Fulton Publishers.

Task 2 Reading

Graham, J & Kelly, A (2000) Reading Under Control, 2nd edn, London: David Fulton Publishers, pp 142–150.

Task 3 Reading

Berger, A, Henderson, J and Morris, D (1999) Implementing the Literacy Hour for Pupils with Learning Difficulties, London: David Fulton Publishers.

Graham, J & Kelly, A (2000) Reading Under Control, 2nd edn, London: David Fulton Publishers, pp 35–42, 144–146.

Books and other resources

DFE Circular 6/94, *Code of Practice on the Identification and Assessment of Special Educational Needs*, London: HMSO.

Farrell, M (2000) *The Special Education Handbook*, 2nd edn, London: David Fulton Publishers.

Graham, J & Kelly, A (2000) Reading Under Control, 2nd edn, London: David Fulton Publishers.

Graham, J & Kelly, A (1998) Writing Under Control, London: David Fulton Publishers.

Chapter 26

Objectives

To be able to plan differentiated learning experiences in which the whole class can work together, and others in which groups of children can work separately.

To be able to set appropriate tasks for children of high ability in English and to be prepared to meet the challenge of 'gifted' children.

Task 1 Reading

OFSTED (1995) *English: a Review of Inspection Findings 1993/94*, London: HMSO, pp 5–10.

Wray, D & Lewis, M (1997) Extending Literacy, London: Routledge, chapter 2.

Audio-visual

DfEE (1998) *Literacy Training Pack, Video 2, Module 4, Sequences 2, 4 & 5; Module 5*, Sequences 1 – 6.

Task 2 Reading

Dean, G (1998) *Challenging the More Able Language User*, London: David Fulton Publishers.

Wray, D & Medwell, J (1998) Teaching English in Primary Schools, London: Letts, pp 25–40.

The lesson plans which you made for the teaching of English during your teaching practice and your evaluations of them.

Task 3 Reading

George, D (1995) *Gifted Education - Identification and Provision*, London: David Fulton Publishers.

Lee-Corbin, H and Denicolo, P (1998) *Recognising and Supporting Able Children in Primary Schools*, London: David Fulton Publishers.

Books and other resources

DfEE (1998) *Literacy Training Pack, Video 2*.

OFSTED (1995) *English: a Review of Inspection Findings* 1993/94, London: HMSO.

Wray, D & Lewis, M (1997) Extending Literacy, London: Routledge.

Wray, D & Medwell, J (1998) Teaching English in Primary Schools, London: Letts.

Chapter 27

Objectives
To be familiar with the methods of statutory assessment in English, how this should be recorded, and the requirements of schools for reporting the results.

Task 1 Reading

Godwin, D & Perkins, M (1998) *Teaching Language and Literacy in the Early Years*, London: David Fulton Publishers, pp 19–20, 24–25, 43–44, 68, 76, 98, 116–126.

Grugeon, E et al. (1998) *Teaching Speaking and Listening in the Primary School*, London: David Fulton Publishers, pp 100–105.

QCA/DfEE (2000) *Curriculum Guidance for the Foundation Stage*, London: QCA.

SCAA (1996) *Desirable Outcomes for Children's Learning on Entering Compulsory Education*, London: DfEE, pp 3, 6–10.

Task 2 Reading

Graham, J & Kelly, A (2000) *Reading Under Control*, 2nd edn, London: David Fulton Publishers, pp 131–132.

Graham, J & Kelly, A (1998) *Writing Under Control*, London: David Fulton Publishers, pp 124–125.

QCA (1999a) *Official National Test Papers*: English and Maths Tests, Key Stage 1, London: The Stationery Office, pp 1–17, *Reading and Comprehension Booklet and Story Book*.

Task 3 Reading

DfEE (2000) *The National Curriculum*, London: HMSO, Attainment Targets pp 1–7.

Graham, J & Kelly, A (2000) *Reading Under Control*, 2nd edn, London: David Fulton Publishers, pp 132–135.

Graham, J & Kelly, A (1998) *Writing Under Control*, London: David Fulton Publishers, pp 118, 125–127.

Grugeon, E et al. (1998) *Teaching Speaking and Listening in the Primary School*, London: David Fulton Publishers, pp 114–116.

QCA (1999b) *Official National Test Papers*: English Tests, Key Stage 2, London: The Stationery Office, pp v–xiii, 3–55 and *Reading Answer Booklet, Writing Test Sheets* and *Reading Book*.

Books and other resources

DfEE (2000) The National Curriculum, London: HMSO.

Godwin, D & Perkins, M (1998) Teaching Language and Literacy in the Early Years, London: David Fulton Publishers.

Graham, J & Kelly, A (2000) Reading Under Control, 2nd edn, London: David Fulton Publishers.

Graham, J & Kelly, A (1998) Writing Under Control, London: David Fulton Publishers.

Grugeon, E et al. (1998) Teaching Speaking and Listening in the Primary School, London: David Fulton Publishers.

QCA (1999a) *Official National Test Papers*: English and Maths Tests, Key Stage 1, London: The Stationery Office.

QCA (1999b) *Official National Test Papers*: English Tests, Key Stage 2, London: The Stationery Office.

QCA/DfEE (2000) *Curriculum Guidance for the Foundation Stage*, London: QCA.

SCAA (1996) *Desirable Outcomes for Children's Learning on Entering Compulsory Education*, London: DfEE.

Wray, D & Medwell, J (1998) Teaching English in Primary Schools, London: Letts.

Useful websites

Basic Skills Agency	www.basic-skills.co.uk
Book Trust	www.booktrust.org.uk
British Dyslexia Association	www.bda-dyslexia.org.uk
British Educational Communications and Technology Agency	www.becta.org.uk
British Educational Suppliers Association	www.besanet.org.uk
British Library	www.bl.uk
David Fulton Publishers	www.fultonpublishers.co.uk
Department for Education and Employment	www.dfee.gov.uk
The Dyslexia Institute	www.dyslexia-inst.org.uk
Federation of Children's Book Groups	www.fcbg.mcmail.com
National Association of Special Educational Needs	www.nasen.org.uk
National Grid for Learning (ngfl)	www.ngfl.gov.uk
National Literacy Association	www.nla.org.uk
The National Literacy Trust	www.literacytrust.org.uk
Parents Information Network	www.pin.org.uk
Pre-School Learning Alliance	www.pre-school.org.uk
Qualifications and Curriculum Authority	www.qca.org.uk
School Library Association	www.sla.org.uk
Standards and Effectiveness Unit	www.standards.dfee.gov.uk
Teacher Training Agency	www.teach-tta.gov.uk

Index